THE COWDREYS

IVO TENNANT

THE COWDREYS

PORTRAIT OF A
CRICKETING FAMILY

S I M O N & S C H U S T E R

LONDON·SYDNEY·NEW YORK·TOKYO·SINGAPORE·TORONTO

First published in Great Britain by
Simon & Schuster Ltd in 1990

Simon & Schuster Ltd
West Garden Place
Kendal Street
London W2 2AQ

Simon & Schuster of Australia Pty Ltd
Sydney

A CIP catalogue record for this book is
available from the British Library
ISBN 0–671–65323–7

Typeset in 11/13 by Selectmove
Printed and bound in Great Britain by
Billing & Sons Ltd, Worcester

Contents

Acknowledgements

The material for what follows is based on the observations of those listed below and on the books subsequently detailed. It is the result of interviews with Colin, Christopher and Graham for *The Times* and *The Cricketer* and on less formal conversations with them over the years. I am grateful to Penny Cowdrey, Colin's first wife, Mrs Ann Glover, her sister, and Carol Keith, Colin's daughter, for their assistance. I should also like to thank the curator of the M.C.C. library at Lord's, Stephen Green, and his assistants for their help and use of the books below; and for the use of *The Times* newspaper and photographic library. There will soon be as many files on Colin Cowdrey as on Winston Churchill.

I should also like to thank the following:

Leslie Ames, C.B.E.; Asif Iqbal; Jack Bailey; Trevor Bailey; John Barclay; Paul Box-Grainger; David Dalby; Mike Denness; Major Martin ffrench Blake; Peter Franklin (Homefield School); Sir Leonard Hutton; Ray Illingworth, C.B.E.; Graham Johnson; David Kemp (Tonbridge School); Nick Kemp; Peter May, C.B.E.; Dudley Moore; Mark Nicholas; Basil D'Oliveira, O.B.E.; Tony Pawson; The R.A.F.; Peter Richardson; Bill Sale; Joffy Sale; Raman Subba Row; Derek Underwood, M.B.E.; John Woodcock; Ian Wooldridge; Tim Wright.

Two individuals requested anonymity.

The following books were consulted: *M.C.C. The Autobiography of a Cricketer* (Hodder and Stoughton); *The Incomparable Game* (Hodder and Stoughton); *Cricket Today* (Arthur Barker); *Time for Reflection* (Frederick Muller); *Tackle Cricket this Way* (Stanley Paul). All by Colin Cowdrey. *Good Enough?* (Pelham) by Chris Cowdrey and Jonathan Smith; *Conflicts in Cricket* (Kingswood) by Jack Bailey; *The Greatest of my Time* (Eyre & Spottiswoode) by Trevor Bailey; *Twin Ambitions* (Stanley Paul) by Alec Bedser; *The Art of Captaincy* (Hodder and Stoughton) by Mike Brearley; *I Don't Bruise Easily*

(MacDonald and James) by Brian Close; *From Bradman to Boycott* (Queen Anne Press) by Ted Dexter; *Swings and Roundabouts* (Pelham) by Graham Dilley; *Captain's Innings* (Stanley Paul) by Keith Fletcher; *Cricket Gallery* (Lutterworth Press) edited by David Frith; *The Cricket Captains of England* (Cassell) by Alan Gibson; *The Heart of Cricket* (Arthur Barker) by Tom Graveney; *Chucked Around* (Pelham) by Charlie Griffith; *Pace like Fire* (Pelham) by Wes Hall; *Bowled Over* (Rigby) by Neil Hawke; *Yorkshire and back* (Queen Anne Press) by Ray Illingworth; *Stumper's View* (Stanley Paul) by Alan Knott; *The History of Kent C.C.C.* (Helm) by Dudley Moore; *The Centurions* (J.M. Dent) by Patrick Murphy; *Inns and Outs* (Pelham) by Norman O'Neill; *The D'Oliveira Affair* (Collins) by Basil D'Oliveira; *Time to Declare* (J.M. Dent) by Basil D'Oliveira; *Runs and Catches* (Faber) by Tony Pawson; *Always ready* (Gary Sparke) by Ian Redpath; *Lord's Taverners Sticky Wicket Book* (Queen Anne Press) by Tim Rice; *As I said at the Time* (Collins Willow) by E.W. Swanton; *Gubby Allen, Man of Cricket* (Hutchinson/Stanley Paul) by E.W. Swanton; *Sort of a Cricket Person* (Collins) by E.W. Swanton; *The World of Cricket* (Michael Joseph) edited by E.W. Swanton; *The Ashes retained* (Evans) by E.M. Wellings. And, of course, various editions of *Wisden*.

Introduction

This is not, contrary to one newspaper report during the course of my research, an authorised biography. If there is ever such a book, it is likely that it will be written not by a journalist or author but by a member of the Cowdrey family.

The original intention was for Christopher Cowdrey and myself to write about leading Kent cricketers, a plan which was discounted on account of the time he needed to expend on his benefit. From that came John Pawsey's idea for this text: for there has not been a biography of Colin or Christopher. It is an unusual subject in that the Cowdreys are an unusual family. From two generations three first-class cricketers have emerged, two of them captains of England, the third yet to realise his full potential. I have known them for more than twenty years and watched and reported on them playing cricket on countless occasions. Their personalities have, to me, been as compelling as their sporting achievements and I have attempted to reflect that interest here: to examine their characters as well as their extra cover drives.

The only claim I make for what follows is that, after conducting 32 interviews and reading numerous books, magazines and newspapers, I have striven to give a fair and balanced account of the personalities and careers of this most renowned of cricketing families. The career of Colin Cowdrey, especially, has been multi-faceted, sometimes seemingly self-contradictory. Their achievements and records are enshrined for ever in *Wisden*: I have tried, if they will excuse the metaphor, to put some flesh on the bones.

Chapter One

The Initial Advantage

WHEN COLIN COWDREY announced his retirement after a quarter of a century of fretting and gambolling his way through Test and county cricket, he hoped – prayed – he would play one last great innings. It was 1975 and the Australians, against whom he had begun and ended his international career, were due shortly at the St. Lawrence ground, Canterbury. When they left, rather later than they had anticipated, they had been beaten – not so much by Kent, as by batting which drove the critics to superlatives. Yet Colin's unbeaten 151 was but one of an extraordinary number of family feats on the cricket field that week: Christopher, Colin's eldest son, made a century and took five wickets for Tonbridge School, which he was captaining. He presented Jeremy, the second son, with his colours. Meanwhile Graham, the youngest, was captaining his preparatory school on the Kent coast and making an indecent number of runs all week. Penny, Colin's first wife and daughter of a distinguished Kent chairman, was achieving her best score, eighteen, in a mothers' match. She was also her side's wicket-keeper. Colin's father, who named his son in the initials of M.C.C., started something, for sure.

Christopher followed his father by captaining Kent and England. One of his tasks was to present Graham with his county cap, at a time when their father had attained high office in the administration of cricket. There have been numerous cricketing families and the Cowdreys were not the first to include two captains of their country. Yet none has been as pre-eminent, nor exhibited quite such a blend of style and statistics.

They attract all manner of adjectives, depending on the bystander's perspective and, seemingly, his geographical base. The outlook is invariably different in the north of England than it is in Kent, where an obsession with the Cowdreys runs right

1

through club and county, to the extent of becoming an almost unhealthy monomania. They are a family who know of their special standing in the game, and can abuse it. They are kind and charming, yet unreliable; diffident yet strong-willed; witty yet moody; overtly confident yet covertly self-doubting. The bottom line is a compelling enthusiasm for cricket. Sport has been the thread running through the Cowdreys for generations: Colin's grandfather was able to field his own family team near his home in Surrey – even the scorer was a relation. They were, and are, extremely competent at most games. They are a solidly middle-class family, and content to remain so. Colin is the exception, but then geniuses, or near-geniuses, always are.

By common consent, Colin possessed an ability with the bat and a technique that was equal to Bradman or Sobers. By common consent also, he did not make full use of his gifts. On the face of it, this is a strange conclusion to draw of a man who played more than a hundred times for England, scored more than a hundred centuries and who often elevated the art of batsmanship. He himself has no answer as to the inconsistencies in his batting, why one day he would take a Test attack apart, and the next flounder against bowlers barely heard of before or since.

His critics have. Once, when Colin was berating Christopher for not having enough confidence – he had just been passed over for the captaincy of Kent in 1982 – his daughter, Carolyn, piped up: 'Dad, every time I read about you in a book it says that if only you had had more confidence you would have done so much more.'

A morass of values, traditions and complexities merge in this deeply perplexing man whose affection for the game and consummate ambition, masked by diffidence, has led him to a position of cricketing influence unparalleled anywhere in the world. When Kent, in spite of being top-heavy with committeemen and administrators, are in need of resolving a local difficulty, the cry goes up: 'Send for Colin.' When the outgoing president of M.C.C. had to nominate his successor for the club's bicentenary year, Colin's standing in the game, and his initials, precluded any other choice. It was his apotheosis. When the International Cricket Council seek someone akin to

The Cowdrey cover-drive, as beautiful a stroke as there can ever have been. (Sport and General)

an ambassador to settle afflictions, he is their man. He is truly the most diplomatic of individuals, a man of infinite charm prepared to brook sages and fools alike. He is prepared to make time if only, as he once wrote, to explain how he is so pushed for time. He is a busy man, who tries to put back into the game as much as he has taken out. He attracts, for his efforts, both praise and cynicism (and quite probably jealousy). 'He is kind to us all, to get us all on his side,' was the estimation of one former colleague, who played with him for many years. A close friend, David Kemp, countered: 'I have seen him show kindnesses to others too often for it to be anything other than genuine. He could not keep up that façade, if it is one, all of the time.' And yet Colin remains imprisoned by his own persona. He would have liked to have been as uninhibited as his eldest son, but his development was arrested by a lonely childhood and school and cricket masters who belonged to a bygone age. Always a guest in someone else's home, through his parents' residing abroad, he became unobtrusive and indecisive to a fault.

Enigma was the bond between person and player. Colin was essentially an amateur who struggled to become a professional. He was not acquisitive on the field and he was restricted by the way he should appear. At the end of the triumphant 1967–68 M.C.C. visit to the West Indies, an England player who was being interviewed by the B.B.C. at the airport cited a slow over-rate as having been a factor in their success. Colin, on overhearing this, terminated the recording.

Trevor Bailey wrote of Colin that 'it is quite inconceivable anyone should dislike him'. Ray Illingworth, a decade later, wrote that 'he was not generally liked by cricketers'. The truth, as ever, appears to lie somewhere in the middle. Many players, especially those from a different background, hardly knew him. He was never 'one of the boys'. They respected him for his great talent, but did not always take him at his word. Colin's dislike of disappointing people has made it hard for him to tell an individual he was being dropped, or to refuse an invitation. The resultant impression, when the team sheet was pinned up, or the engagement cancelled by Colin at the eleventh hour, was one of unreliability. This characteristic, in the view of certain colleagues and opponents, extended to inconsistencies at the crease over 'walking'.

The most general criticism of Colin's career, though, attaches itself to his captaincy. Coming from an educated background he was expected, in the 1950s and 1960s, to be a leader. This applied to both Kent and England. The experiment with a professional, Len Hutton, proved to be successful, but thereafter the selectors reverted to the traditional amateur. The next four captains of England, Peter May, Colin himself, Ted Dexter and Mike Smith, all came from Oxbridge backgrounds. It was only when they had retired, were injured or were adjudged to have failed, that captains such as Brian Close and Ray Illingworth, both the very antithesis of Colin, were enlisted. There is no doubt that Colin would have had greater peace of mind had he eschewed the captaincy of his country altogether. Yet, to him, that would have been tantamount to neglect of duty.

For a decade, the decade in which his batting should have been predominant, the England captaincy was tossed to him and then repeatedly snatched away, as if he were an aberrant child. He did not complain; his upbringing, Christian nature and rectitude precluded that. Not for him a great outpouring in the popular press. He underplayed himself. He was prepared to accept impositions which others would have found intolerable. He was a loyal vice-captain to May, Dexter and Smith, but found it hard to stomach being asked to tour Australia for a fourth time as vice-captain. He accepted, ultimately, to deputise for Illingworth. He could not win. Had he refused, he would have been charged with disloyalty to the captain and begun the tour on the wrong footing. By accepting, he was obliged – theoretically – to work closely with a man who was antipathetic to him.

He can also be said to have been dogged by ill-fortune. After all, he had deputised constantly for May and, statistically, with reasonable success. The assumption had been that he would, in due course, be rewarded. He could justifiably have assumed that Illingworth was only standing in for him after he snapped an Achilles tendon. His triumphant tour of the West Indies was still remembered, a tour in which he had won the Wisden Trophy and shown that, given a free rein, his captaincy and his batting prospered in tandem.

The differences between Colin and Ray Illingworth stemmed from the envy and distrust that always existed between professionals and amateurs, especially those with Oxbridge backgrounds. The distinction in English cricket was officially abolished in 1962 yet the usage of the words and, for a while, the traditions, were continued. That winter it was the former amateur cricketers, including Colin, who dined at the Duke of Norfolk's table. The Cowdreys were, and still are, regarded as the epitome of privilege within cricket spheres. In addition to being envied for his talent, his background and his connections, Colin was known not to have had to struggle materially. His father-in-law, Stuart Chiesman, was not only chairman of

Kent for the best part of the fifteen years when Colin was their captain. Chiesman was also his employer and benefactor (although it is fair to say Colin would not have been so well-remunerated as a director of Chiesman's had he not been a notable cricketer). Chiesman was a magnate and would not have wasted his company's money: Colin offered his firm much in the way of public relations, just as he did to Barclays Bank after his retirement. A directorship of Chiesman's, a group of departmental stores in Kent, enabled Colin to be independent of his county committee in a way that no captain, his eldest son included, is today. It heightened his power and influence. When Leslie Ames was taken on, firstly as manager and then as secretary-manager, it was at Colin's instigation. Ames was not so much employed by Kent as by Colin and Chiesman.

Power and influence. Colin enjoyed both, and was attracted to those who possessed them. He was, and is, socially ambitious to an extent that his family were not and are not. His host of friends and acquaintances ranged from Prime Ministers in Sir Robert Menzies, Sir Alec Douglas-Home and Ted Heath, to luminaries such as Field Marshall Montgomery and the Duke of Norfolk. The Duke, who was especially fond of Colin, presented him with uniforms which he loved to inspect and stroke. Driving from one match to another, Colin would sometimes go miles out of his way to see some illustrious individual. On occasion he would arrive unannounced, which could be embarrassing for all concerned. Yet he was a good guest in that, such incidents excepted, his manners were beyond reproach. He is a prodigious letter writer and makes much use of the telephone. He enjoys sending congratulatory notes and messages, and maintains his own secretary to assist him in doing so. He prepares speeches meticulously and is practised at the art. He is quite able, on sensing the atmosphere at a formal event, to adapt his lines accordingly. Christopher and Jeremy, his elder sons, have inherited this ability.

In retirement from playing, immersed in administration, he keeps in touch with former colleagues. Those whom he does not see at committee meetings, or who do not mix in his social circles, do not contact him: they are contacted by him. Colin maintains a patrician interest in what they are doing and, on account of his connections the world over, has been able to introduce a number of them to prospective employers. His capacity for sending congratulatory notes is matched only by his predilection for sitting on committees.

When a group of contemporary players come together, as they are wont to do at dinners and commemorative occasions, it is Colin Cowdrey, the man, they tend to discuss, not Colin Cowdrey, the cricketer. It is evidence of the complexities of his nature and the influence he wields. Yet, in the mind's eye, it is not in that capacity that those who saw him play see him now. They do not picture him as president of M.C.C. nor chairman of I.C.C., nor in any capacity other than on a cricket field. They see the Cowdrey cover-drive, as beautiful a stroke as there has ever been. The face of the bat is open, the ball bisects the ring of fielders before gathering pace and coming to rest at the foot of the old tree at Canterbury. A change in the field placings, and there is a different target, this time a boundary board. The maddening thing for everyone else on the field was that he expected to hit it.

Just how good a cricketer he was remains, of course, a subjective judgement. His figures and records are enshrined for ever in *Wisden*. Only a very good batsman averages more than 40 in Test cricket; and only an exceptional batsman scores a century of centuries. When comparisons are made, as they are frequently, Peter May is regarded as the greatest batsman since the War, Colin as a great player and Ted Dexter as a player of great innings. The rider with Colin was that when he went out to bat on a firm pitch with the sun shining and his side well-positioned, he thought he would make a decent score, yet often failed. In trying circumstances, when he would have given anything to be on the golf course, he almost invariably succeeded.

He was among the best-loved of sportsmen by the general public. Once established, no cricketer in modern times was accorded a greater reception on going in to bat. Crowds empathised with him – they appreciated the way he batted, admired his courage against the quickest bowling and his stoicism in the face of adversity, sympathised with his disappointments. Above all, they sensed his commitment to the game. If they were less appreciative of him in the north of

England than at Lord's or Melbourne, it reflected a different approach to the game. No-one could accuse Colin of possessing the characteristics of a Yorkshireman although, if he had, or if he had been dependent on cricket for his livelihood, the statistics would have been still more impressive.

He was never one to be consumed by averages. Yet only eleven batsmen have scored more than his 42,719 runs in the history of the game; only one English batsman, Geoffrey Boycott, has exceeded his 7,624 runs in Test cricket; no English batsman has outstripped his 22 Test hundreds or 114 Test appearances; the number of catches he took in Test cricket, 120, originally a world record, remains a record for an English fielder. It is quite conceivable that, had he recaptured the Ashes in 1970–71, he would have been knighted, rather than receiving, as he did, the C.B.E. With statistics like that, it remains a wonder that any of Colin's three sons should want to follow him into first-class cricket. They were percipient enough to realise that they had little chance of emulating him.

Christopher, Jeremy and Graham were given every chance to play cricket, both at school and in the sizeable garden of a large home on the borders of Kent and Surrey. Their sister, Carol (as she is known) was given every chance to bowl and field; their mother, Penny, every opportunity of utilising her washing machine; and their dog every possibility of breaking its neck in pursuit of skiers. Colin was one of the first to install a bowling machine in his garden, having one specially imported from Australia after he had his left arm broken by Wes Hall. Even in 1963 this earliest of models patented by an American firm could deliver a ball as fast as Hall. In due course a hard net was installed. There were excellent facilities, too, for various other sports.

So it was as well that Penny appreciated cricket. Indeed, she enjoyed it almost as much as her father did. Quick-witted and determined, she liked to have her own way. But she saw herself as an underdog, someone who was yoked to cricket. Uncomplainingly she ferried the boys to matches all round southern England whilst Colin was unavoidably detained elsewhere. It was inevitable that the children grew closer to her than to their father, who was away summer and winter, Christmas Day and sports day. When the marriage fell apart

Practice makes perfect: heading for the lawn at Kentish Border, Colin with (left to right) Graham (5), Carol (8), Jeremy (10) and Christopher (12). (Keystone Press Agency)

it came as a surprise to cricket followers, who were shocked that Colin had left home; yet the fact that he had been away so much had, if anything, held their relationship together. His absences were reckoned by friends to have merely postponed the split, since he and Penny were very disparate people.

For Christopher, given his second name of Stuart after his maternal grandfather, it was a question of whether he could make a name for himself through his own ability, or whether he would be unable to escape the pressures of his surname. Had he inherited his father's self-doubt and more depressive tendencies, it is conceivable he would have lasted only a few years in county cricket. It was never likely that he was going to be as good as his father and the comparisons, from supporters and Press alike, were sometimes overwhelming. If he scored a century, it was only to be expected. If he was out without scoring, well, how could he have been with his background? They vexed him sufficiently to pose the question *Good Enough*? as the title of his book after he had played for England. Asif Iqbal, his first captain, said, 'He was fortunate that nature blessed him with a fine outgoing personality, his father's sense of humour and an openness which his father did not possess.' It was not long before he discovered kindred spirits in his own dressing-room and in others up and down the land – yet the comparisons did not abate.

In 1978, the year after Christopher made his debut for Kent, his parents split up. It was but one of many estrangements in Britain that year: divorce was becoming commonplace. This, though, was different. For a start, it was news which made the front pages of national newspapers. It was not an amicable parting. A former England cricket captain, regarded as a pillar of moral rectitude, had left home for a daughter of the Duke of Norfolk, a former head of the Roman Catholic church.

The children sided with their mother. She was the parent left behind. She was the one they knew. To this day Penny lives in the hope that Colin will return: he remains 'my husband' even though they are divorced and Colin is married to Lady Anne Herries of Terregles. The children do not share her optimism. They look after her and they do not invite Lady Anne to their weddings. Penny retains her affection for her sons and has grown closer to her daughter. She remains a constant spectator at Kent grounds. It is a puzzle to her that Colin, when he is also present, stays on the farthest boundary.

Colin is passionately committed to fostering a good relationship with Christopher. He is conscious of the coldness that existed between them after he left Penny, and is, he says, 'relieved' that all four children have carved out niches for themselves. Of the four, he remains closest to Jeremy, a stockbroker, whose cricket stresses the social niceties of the game, rather than his personal average. Carol, his daughter, whose own individuality was rather submerged by cricket and four men for many years, made her presence felt through her own ebullience. Her insecurities, which surfaced in the class-room, have been quelled by maturity and marriage. Graham, who was fourteen when his parents split up, was the most profoundly affected. Of the three sons, he, who does not know his father especially well, has probably found it hardest to come to terms with being a Cowdrey.

The aspect of the personalities of Colin and his three sons which is not readily apparent is determination. Graham Johnson, whose career with Kent took in both generations, calls it 'steely ambition'. The sons have had to push themselves harder than Colin, who could fall back on a sublime talent and material comfort, and who saw at an early age that those whose efforts were visibly forced were not necessarily those who succeeded. Not that Christopher, Jeremy or Graham would wish to be seen to be pushing themselves. It would be foreign to their upbringing.

Christopher's ambitions have, unusually, stretched to cap-taincy rather than merely playing. From his first seasons in county cricket it was evident he would not be an exceptional performer. Indeed, he struggled for several years to hold down a regular first-team place. He became a 'bits and pieces' player who was of greater value to his side in one-day than in three-day cricket. He could bat a bit, bowl a bit and energise colleagues in the field. At the age of 22, well before he had established himself, he had one special ambition. He wanted to captain Kent.

When he came to it, the circumstances were controversial. The senior players preferred the more analytical style of the deposed captain, Chris Tavaré. There were concerns that Christopher had been appointed because of who he was, not what he was. Nevertheless, it was his success with Kent that led to his captaining England. It had seemed that his Test career, such as it was, was over. Then, with England struggling against a far stronger West Indies side, and captains falling by the wayside, the chairman of selectors turned to Christopher. He was being asked to retrieve a lost cause, just as Colin had been against the same Test opposition in 1966 – and he was in an invidious position. For he had been appointed by his own godfather, which the predators were quick to seize on. 'Poor old Chris,' said Colin. 'I know what hell this can be.'

It proved to be nothing less. Having stated that 'Christopher's style of captaincy is what we now need,' the selectors were soon behaving as if they had said nothing of the sort. After England had been soundly beaten, Christopher was precluded from playing in the final Test through injury; and then he discovered, as his father had once before him, that the stand-in captain retained the job. Then, Colin retreated into himself, his game and his peace of mind shattered by the appointment of Illingworth to lead M.C.C. in Australia. This was not Christopher's way. He chose, as the vehicle of his frustration, to the chagrin of his father, his godfather and the Kent committee, *The Sun*. It was not, in normal circumstances, a newspaper they would take. Now, they were hard put to avoid it.

Christopher's disaffection manifested itself further the following year, when he signed to join the unofficial England tour of South Africa. His father was also about to take up a post – the chairmanship of the International Cricket Council. He would have to deal with politicians and cricket officials who, to say the least, would not be enamoured that his son was running into the arms of the pariahs of the game. It would hardly enhance their relationship. Yet Christopher, as ever, was his own man.

As captain of Kent, Christopher's concerns have been compounded by an additional difficulty over selection. It is, namely, whether or not to select his youngest brother, Graham. This has been made more problematic by Graham's not having established himself as a county cricketer.

Graham has, or was thought to have, a greater natural ability than Christopher. Those who were at Tonbridge with him recall him decimating bowlers. It was assumed from an early age that he would play first-class cricket: in retrospect he felt he was pushed into it, though not by his parents. He made an immediate impact, scoring a half-century against the 1985 Australians and the following season proving his worth in the one-day game. The pundits thought they were watching an England batsman in the making. In the Benson and Hedges Cup final of 1986 he showed, in almost leading Kent to victory, that there was something of Colin's temperament in his game. Not that he plays in anything like the same manner. Like Christopher he has become – perhaps obliged to become – predominantly a one-day cricketer. He works the ball to leg, clouts it off the back foot past cover and is quite prepared to hit over the top. Not for him is there the opportunity of playing himself in for half an hour as his father was able to do in another era.

There is much more to Graham than meets the eye. His progress as a cricketer has, it would seem, been impeded by his insecurities as a human being. He, of all the brothers and their sister, feels the pressure of being a Cowdrey the most. Well-meaning and possessing his mother's openness, he yet finds it hard to trust outsiders. He escapes the harsh world of professional sport through finding solace in religion, the music of the Irish pop singer, Van Morrison, whose concerts he has attended an inordinate number of times, and books. He tries to forge for himself a different identity to Christopher, just as Christopher had tried to become distinct from his father.

If Graham is the most determined of the three sons, Jeremy, who is two years younger than Christopher and five years older than Graham, is perhaps the strongest character. He was born with less ability for playing games than his brothers, but that was counterpointed by his being the cleverest academically. Whereas at school Christopher would dream up every possible excuse to avoid the classroom and take to the nets, Jeremy, without the same sporting prowess, needed less inducement to work. Initially, though, he would have liked to have been a cricketer. In the school summer holidays Christopher and he played from ten to four each day, a palmy existence from which Graham was excluded. He was deemed not to be up to their standard.

Nevertheless, there is a bond between them. 'People think we are rivals, but we have a good relationship,' said Jeremy. He is counselled by Christopher and is protective towards Graham. He follows the brothers' progress avidly, watches them when he can and was largely responsible for his firm of stockbrokers, James Capel, sponsoring Kent for four years.

He is particularly close to Carol and, since they live a six hit or two apart in Clapham, south London, sees more of her than Christopher or Graham. 'Jeremy and I are different from our brothers because we are in secure professions,' she said. She runs her own promotions company from home, where the sitting-room is dominated by a lithograph of a painting from the Long Room at Lord's, 'Tossing for innings'. It was a present from her father. Try as she may, and she tried for much of her formative life, there is no escaping cricket. The game embraced her even after her days as a bowler on the lawn were over. She worked for a while at the Oval and when she went abroad, her surname was recognised. In Australia she was fêted. She settled, when she married, not far from the Oval, yet she will not go there. She dislikes the place. She will watch Christopher and Graham at Lord's and not relax until they have scored 20 runs apiece: her nervousness is inherited from her mother. In time she has grown to enjoy the game because her brothers are involved, and will even admit now to 'loving' cricket.

It remains to be seen whether the Cowdreys can unearth a third generation first-class cricketer or whether, as with other families, the lineal descent takes diverse directions. There is no doubting, though, that future offspring will be given every opportunity to play any number of games and of these, cricket will be to the fore. In 1977, when Christopher was making his way, John Woodcock wrote in *The Times*: 'Should you be thinking of staging a pentathlon, the Cowdrey garden is the place to go.' It is a fair bet that this will still be the case in the years to come.

Chapter Two

A Rare Talent

C OLIN'S MIDDLE-CLASS, colonial upbringing in India in the 1930s was typical for the times. His father, Ernest Cowdrey, was a useful cricketer to the point that he considered he could make a career of his talent. At Whitgift in Croydon, a middle-ranking public school, he had illusions of all-round prowess at the game. His own father, who was also educated there and who worked for John Dickinson, the paper manufacturer, was keen on sport, tennis in particular; and father and son both turned out for a Cowdrey XI which competed on a cramped ground in Sanderstead, Surrey. Colin's great-aunt was the scorer.

Ernest Cowdrey's father's work for John Dickinson took him to India and, indeed, various Cowdreys were born there. There was, too, already a Kentish connection: he owned a bungalow on the coast at Pevensey. Ernest was expected to follow his father into his firm but chose instead to attempt a variety of other professions before settling for tea planting. He spent five years in India before returning to England and marrying Molly Taylor, to whom he had been engaged throughout that period. She, too, was fond of sport. They had met at a cricket club – which might explain why she did not demur at Ernest's whimsical choice of initials for her only child, a choice which has, perhaps, a simple explanation. Ernest was a frustrated cricketer in that his talent did not quite match his ambition. His cricket career peaked when he was selected for a European XI against M.C.C. at Madras Cricket Club during M.C.C.'s tour of 1926–7. Listed as 'Cowdray' in the score book, which is retained at the Oval, he batted at number seven and made 48 in a drawn match. He was bowled by Ewart Astill, the former Leicestershire cricketer, who had not done with the Cowdreys. He was to play a rather more significant role in their lives when he coached Colin at Tonbridge.

In his son, Ernest saw unmistakable talent. Born on 24 December 1932, Colin was soon initiated in the intricacies of cricket on a tea plantation 200 miles from Bangalore. There was no shortage of servants to assist with this education: in *Time for Reflection* he tells of how an Indian boy eight years older would play cricket or golf all day with him on the tennis court in the garden of their small bungalow. Ernest would venture out of his office on the estate to oversee his son's progress and to try to ensure Colin's game was as technically correct as it could be for a child. Rather than attempt to belt the ball out of sight, as is the natural inclination of a boy, Colin would attempt to impress him by defending his wicket at all costs. It was one of the rules of their own game that the bat was given up once the batsman was out. There was no reprieve. Ernest was also a disciplinarian in that he tried to eliminate the cow shot from Colin's game. Indeed, he succeeded, since Colin was given out to any shot he played to leg.

On the tennis court Colin was beginning to develop a technique, driving the hard ball (not a cricket ball) back towards the bowler or into the off-side. Every so often he would be told to oil and clean his bat; if he remonstrated, saying that he would rather ride his bicycle, he would be chided. A real cricketer, one who played for England, would always have to do this. Ironically, several years later, the first shot Colin saw on his initial visit to Lord's was a cow shot – by none other than Wally Hammond.

Colin inherited characteristics from his father other than just a love of games. Quintessentially they were a certain chubbiness, a round, sallow face and small hands. Ernest, too, was moody, had a sense of humour and a weak heart. Like Colin and, most vividly, Christopher, Ernest's transparent enthusiasm for sport never waned, not even in relative isolation on the sub-continent. Colin was to inherit his means of transmitting that enthusiasm.

This boyish, infectious joy was evident when parents and child were returning to England by sea in 1938. At Port Said they were overtaken by the ship bringing the Australians for the start of another tour. On board was the captain, one Don Bradman, invisible since he and the ship, silhouetted on the horizon, were some three miles away and fast disappearing;

yet Ernest whisked Colin out of his cabin and hauled him on to the rails to show him this wondrous sight. It was an image which left an indelible mark on Colin, then aged five, and was the start of a conventional education away from his parents. They were to spend that summer with him, but it was only a temporary departure from estrangement. They were back in India that autumn, Ernest having absorbed as much Test cricket as he could in between playing in games himself.

In one respect, the start of Colin's schooling had been anything but conventional. His father had written to the headmaster of Homefield, the preparatory school he was to attend at Sutton, Surrey, asking if Colin could join in the junior cricket game the summer term before he was due to attend as a day boy. The headmaster, Charles Walford, assented to this to the bemusement of other pupils; he was a schoolmaster of the kind who believed strongly in the Victorian ideal that an education applied as much to the body as to the mind.

Walford part owned the school and ran it for 40 years until his death. Large and shy, he determined to make it the best in the neighbourhood. He had his prejudices – the sons of retail trade were not considered *personae gratae* – and he introduced the cane. Old boys remarked, once safely out of his grasp, that with such a powerful headmaster, strong discipline from others was completely unnecessary. His standard punishment, since the cane was used principally for extreme indiscipline or bad work, was detention at noon or on Saturday afternoons. And yet he engendered affection as well as respect. Graham Sutherland, the artist, remembered him as 'a man both awesome and tender'. Another old boy said that 'he *was* the school, a completely dedicated schoolmaster. He was a brilliant teacher and the finest games coach I have known.' To Colin, he was just about the most ruthless man he ever met. Certainly Homefield was regarded as one of the leading prep schools in the area, for sons of professional fathers who went on, in the main, to Dulwich, Epsom, St. Paul's and Tonbridge rather than Eton, Harrow or Winchester.

Colin was to live in the holidays with his maternal grandparents or with his uncle, another keen cricketer, just a mile from Sutton. Without ceremony his parents left him there and set off again for India: such partings were unemotional even when, as in this instance, the Cowdreys would not be seeing their boy again for several years. When Colin came out of school to be met by his grandmother, he was told that his parents had 'gone to work'. He was not, in fact, to see them for seven years; for the following year war broke out.

Already an only child, Colin increasingly had to provide his own entertainment when not at school; living in a world of adults he had no option. He spent much of his time in the holidays at the farm of another uncle near Leicester and much of his free time playing with a ball. For so long as he had one in his possession, he was content.

Walford, as with Ernest, swiftly recognised a rare talent. He had a determination to make something, or a somebody, of every boy who came under his influence. A rugby Blue, he also wallowed in cricket and would watch over the school games in the afternoon. He even organised playground cricket, forcing the boys to play the ball along the ground. He taught classics and football, and did not spare himself from the rigid discipline that he wished to impose on others. He was, it was said, the martinet who instilled the purity in Colin's character.

Since discipline at Homefield was of paramount importance, it extended to the cricket fields which the boys themselves watered, rolled and marked out. A boy's ability was fostered by constant practice. So when Colin scored a century – or so it was thought – in the first proper game in which he played, Walford's attention was accentuated. The circumstances were bizarre, not least because he had been chosen for the under-eleven side as a wicket-keeper-batsman. Engrossed in his own innings, he was made aware that he was on the verge of a milestone when shouts of encouragement winged their way out to him in the middle. 'Seven more!' and then 'Five more!' was followed by ecstatic cheering when Colin completed the runs that he, and everyone else, thought had brought him a century. Small boys on the outfield turned cartwheels.

Colin, remembering having seen a photograph of Len Hutton raising his bat at the Oval in 1938 in acclamation of the applause, merrily waved his. Conscious even at his age of the style and spirit in which he thought the game was played, he then threw his wicket away as Jack Hobbs might have done. Yards down the pitch, he gave an easy stumping chance and

18

ran into bear hugs from school friends on the boundary. Minutes later his unrestrained joy was ruined when his runs were counted again to ensure there had been no error. It transpired that he had made only 93. Most of the boys saw the funny side and the master in charge of the game was unsympathetic; Colin, as any small boy would be, was mortified. He was not, after that, inclined to give his wicket away lightly.

There was, though, a pleasing sequel. Walford had missed the innings but, on his return to Homefield, he wrote to Hobbs who had retired a decade before, and who now had a sports business in Fleet Street. Hobbs wrote back to Colin in meticulous longhand: 'Please accept my heartiest congratulations. It is a pity you could get nobody to stay long enough to get your hundred, but I hear you are very keen on the game so I feel sure you will score many centuries in the years to come. I shall watch your career with interest and I wish you the very best of health and fortune.' He sent a size four bat, then worth 25 shillings. Walford, the delighted headmaster, read out the letter at the school's speech day, presenting both that and the miniature bat to Colin. Years later, Colin produced the letter to show an amused Hobbs who, true to his word, had indeed shown considerable interest in his doings. The two met at the Oval when Colin played there for Kent and remained in contact until Hobbs' death in 1963.

Soon after the presentation of Hobbs' bat, Colin was moved to another prep school. The reason was not to do with Walford's curriculum, even if Colin did admit in later years to having been over-shackled; it was because World War Two was raging overhead. When Croydon was bombed, Colin's grandparents decided that he should be educated in the safer environment of Bognor Regis – and it was two years before he was to return to Homefield.

When this duly occurred, Walford's greeting was a cold one. He summoned Colin to the nets where he swiftly informed him that there were technical failings in his play and that he should have to begin all over again. Walford included him in the 1st XI game, although it was not clear whether this was intended to do something about his confidence, or to put him in his place, or both. At any rate, after being bowled four times he was summarily put back into the junior game. Yet Walford it was

19

Back at Homefield as an England batsman. Colin used a bat cut to two and a half inches wide for the Old Boys against the school in 1964. He made 77. (The Times *photo library)*

who helped develop Colin's technique to the extent that, when he left Homefield in 1946, he could play every shot. For a boy of thirteen it was a rare accomplishment, and he was to work hard at perfecting it. He was also, for his age, a most competent bowler of leg-breaks and googlies. He had been taught the art by the Sutton groundsman, Ken Harman, and in his last term, having given up wicket-keeping, he twice took a hat-trick in addition to scoring two centuries.

Colin was, in fact, a better bowler than batsman when he left Homefield, and it was his leg-breaks and googlies which won him a place in Tonbridge's 1st XI at the age of thirteen. He found the comparatively smaller cricket ball, as used by schoolboys, easier to spin. That his bowling did not develop as he grew older was, he felt, because he was simply not good enough. In retirement he said that his bowling lacked 'bottle', which for one who applied himself fully to the rigours of batsmanship was surprising.

Colin left Homefield at an unusual time in the academic calendar. His parents, whom he had not seen for seven years, came back to England on a troopship at the end of the war and, before embarking once again for India, were keen to see their son safely installed at his public school. Ernest had planned that Colin should go to Marlborough in Wiltshire, but that did not materialise since it was full for the start of the summer term. There was a vacancy, though, at Tonbridge, where a new house was opening. So it was there that Colin was sent, to the chagrin of Walford who understandably wanted to retain his star cricketer for one last summer term. The carrot he dangled was the Homefield batting cup: it had not been awarded to Colin in the hope that he would stay on at the school for an additional summer term. Had he done so, it is likely Colin would have broken virtually every prep school record in the book. As it was, he was selected for Tonbridge that very summer, almost as soon as he had entered the school. Colin felt Walford never forgave him, and although he came to watch him play in later years – his proudest moment was when he went to Lord's to watch Colin captain Tonbridge and another old boy lead Clifton – he did not seek Colin out before his death in 1953. 'He would have wanted to put his arm round Colin and he might have felt that that would have been more than Colin could take in public,' said Peter Franklin, a contemporary who inherited Colin's first pair of pads and his collection of stamps from India.

To this day, Colin retains an affection for Homefield. It still has an allure for him. He has returned to play cricket and was a founder member and then chairman of the old boys association, and in 1986 became president of their sports hall appeal. Walford, too, has retained a place in his affections, even if there has been no escaping his inculcation. He gave Colin a sound education, not least on the cricket field. What he omitted was praise of any kind. Consequently Colin was not to know that he was one of the pick, probably the pick, of all child cricketers ever to have played the game in England. His confidence was under-nourished.

Walford notwithstanding, in the Easter holidays before going to Tonbridge Colin's self-esteem was boosted. He was reconciled with his parents and had a fortnight in the Sandham-Gover cricket school in London where, away from Walford's beady eye, he batted with a greater freedom. The sages who patrolled the indoor nets were duly impressed and wrote accordingly to Astill at Tonbridge. They told him to expect a thirteen-year-old of precocious ability, one who could immediately be put into the 1st XI.

Having passed his common entrance exam, Colin arrived at Tonbridge on a Friday evening in April, with the weekend before him in which to unpack and settle in. The following day all the cricketers with the exception of the new boys, the Novi as they were known, went into the nets. Colin, out of curiosity, sat behind them and watched, whereupon Astill spotted him and invited him to bowl. It made for an incongruous sight: here was a small boy in grey flannels, supposed to be neither seen nor heard, parading with his elders and betters decked out in whites. They were prefects and seniors for whom he would shortly be fagging and, inevitably, one of the masters in an adjoining net did not approve. Colin slunk away and, on the Monday morning, thought his punishment was complete when his name was excluded from those forming the junior teams. He was moving away from the notice boards when he discovered he had been listed for the colts game.

In his first practice match he was out without scoring and failed to take a wicket, but the following Saturday he made amends for a further duck with a spell of bowling that brought him four wickets. He kept his place in the team and was promoted on account of sickness and other school commitments to play for the 3rd XI in a practice game against the 2nd XI. He took 16 wickets in two innings and, batting at number eleven, reached double figures.

Great consternation followed: should the fag play with the prefects in the 1st XI? It was decided that he should. Opinion was divided, just as it was when Colin's sons were promoted out of their age groups some three decades later. At some other public schools it would not have happened. At Tonbridge they took a chance and in so doing shaped him, as Walford had done, as an undemonstrative cricketer. Colin's housemaster, James McNeill, simply told him to perform to the best of his ability and not to let him down. And he treated Colin no differently from other boys of the same age group in the house.

So Colin played against the Free Foresters, who included in their illustrious side Gubby Allen, whose Test career was not yet over. Colin, chosen for his slow bowling, went wicketless and, batting at number nine, was out for a duck. On walking back to the pavilion, he was conscious of many in the large crowd melting away. Yet he was retained for Tonbridge's next match and took fourteen Malvern wickets and made ten runs. Gradually after that he moved up the order, but it was through his bowling that he commanded a place in the side. Already able to bowl the googly, he gained several of his wickets through beating the batsman in the air and having him stumped. At that age he was of a height which made it easier to throw the ball up; by the time he left school he had grown noticeably, had lost the art of flight and was intent on pushing the ball through.

There were two memorable occasions as Colin stealthily moved up the order and gained a plentiful haul of wickets during that summer term. One was against Cranbrook when he took a hat-trick and nine wickets in the innings. The other was when he made a duck against Haileybury and was ticked off for showing his disapproval of the umpire's decision to give him out leg before. John Knott, a Kent cricketer and master in charge of the game at Tonbridge, reminded the 1st XI at a special meeting that this was not the way to play. Cricket, he stressed, was different from other games.

So it was, as Colin was rapidly discovering. The climax to Tonbridge's season was their annual encounter with Clifton, one of several schools matches to be played at Lord's before fixture congestion became such that only the Eton versus Harrow encounter was retained. Batting first wicket down, Colin, thought to be the youngest player ever to appear there, scored 75 and 44, and took eight wickets for 117 runs. It merited mentions in both *The Times* and *Wisden*. Coming from a boy of thirteen it was a remarkable achievement, and it helped Tonbridge to win by two runs.

For Colin, the match was significant also in that it was the first time he experienced a form of tension beforehand which was more severe than mere butterflies or nerves. Perversely, it was beneficial to his batting, as it was throughout his career. He cites several of his greatest innings as having been played in adversity or when he was badly injured. At Canterbury in Kent's Gillette Cup semi-final against Sussex in 1967, Alan Dixon, his vice-captain, had to tell him to go in to bat. The 60-over game was not to his liking at the best of times – which these were not. He was struggling with injuries and would have been quite content to have missed the match altogether or to have batted down the order. As with Geoffrey Boycott, in many ways his complete opposite, he needed to be told just how good he was.

He batted that day at Canterbury as positively and with as much élan as he can ever have done. He made 78 and won the match award and the headlines. 'One-day glory of Cowdrey,' the papers called it, and not for the first time. A similar story applied to most of his other outstanding innings: in Colombo, in his first match on tour for M.C.C.; his century and 97 against West Indies on the 1959–60 M.C.C. tour; his hundredth hundred. They could well have been fused by the extra concentration required, for these were all played at times when he was not fit or not keen to play or simply out of form. Colin, in spite of his great commitment to the game, was not a seven-days-a-week cricketer. In that sense he was no Boycott, just as he was not devoted to the mere accumulation of runs. He genuinely preferred a technical challenge to the opportunity of piling up a large score on a flat pitch; that he regarded as a pointless exercise. It partly explained why he did not score a mountain of runs in county cricket.

At Tonbridge, his sheer talent for all ball games made him proficient on the rackets and squash courts, and on the golf course. He had also been effective at boxing at Homefield, and not least had shown nimbleness of feet. He won the under-sixteen public schools rackets competition at Queens Club – he was taught by the omniscient Knott – and when at Oxford reached the final of the amateur rackets championship, also at Queens. He became adept at placement of a squash ball, which as he grew older and heavier (his appetite was prodigious) held him in good stead. Alan Knott recollects hours of running around a squash court while Colin hardly moved. On the Croham Hurst golf course at Croydon he went round one day in 59, which remains a record. He was also a competent rugby player, captaining Tonbridge's junior colts, colts and finally the 1st XV. Only as a cox in the school regatta and at cross-country running, which he found to have no purpose, did Colin not excel.

Strangely, his cricket did not progress after his exceptional start in 1946 as might have been expected. In 1947 he finished with a tally of 37 wickets but his batting fell away, his average dropping from 23 to sixteen. This improved considerably the following year, when he headed both the batting and bowling averages, taking 47 wickets; yet he was not over-pleased. As in 1947, he was unable to repeat the batting of his first match against Clifton at Lord's. Tonbridge lost for the second year in succession.

This was not, though, of such overriding concern as was an injury Colin suffered in that same summer of 1948. He had long been afflicted by pain from kicking a football and this was accentuated when, before going to Tonbridge, he was struck on a toe by a quickish bowler. The pain continued intermittently during his first three years at the school and ultimately became too severe to be ignored any longer. He was sent to a specialist who diagnosed Hallux rigidus, which was an arthritic condition causing stiffening of the toe joints. A course of electrical treatment with hot wax footbaths was prescribed, and three mornings a week in the autumn term Colin was given special permission to attend Pembury hospital. Yet it did not prove to be a cure. The decision was taken to carry out an operation, not, strangely enough, during the holidays but in the spring term. It would not, no doubt, have taken place in the summer, for even then a career as a cricketer was thought to be in the offing.

The operation was successful. Colin's feet, which came under scrutiny from students at a lecture given by the specialist, John Mayer, recovered in the Tonbridge sanatorium where their owner was made to continue with his studies. It was conceivable at the time that a further operation would be necessary; but on removal of the plaster this was discounted. Yet Colin was never entirely free from pain thereafter and his toes were to become almost as notorious as Denis Compton's knee when he came to be examined for entry to the R.A.F. But they were not to be an impediment to his sporting activities at Tonbridge, or to the career he was intent on pursuing.

Further treatment followed at Pembury during the Easter holidays before Colin was fit enough to lead Tonbridge for the first time in the summer term of 1949. He was fitted with a special cricket shoe designed to give protection to the toes, a type which he continued to wear when in discomfort in later years in first-class cricket. That the operation had been worthwhile was evidenced by his best season to date for the 1st XI: 893 runs, an average of 55 and 49 wickets at thirteen apiece. In Tonbridge's second match Colin dispelled any residual fears by making a century and taking five wickets; against a strong Buccaneers side he made the highest score by a Tonbridge boy for 40 years – an unbeaten 181 which won the match. He was now opening the innings, which he disliked less then than he did later: he made further centuries against Haileybury and Old Tonbridgians. Against Clifton at Lord's he reverted to the middle order and two lowly scores in a crushing defeat. His performances overall ensured a place in the Southern Schools XI versus The Rest, in which he made 85. For the Public Schools XI against Combined Universities he took five wickets including that of Peter May – for the first and last time.

Knott, Colin's cricket master, had introduced him to Kent cricket by arranging for him to have three matches for Kent Young Amateurs the previous summer. He had been conspicuously successful, scoring 157, 87 and, against Surrey Young Amateurs, 79. This last innings gave him especial delight since he had had two unproductive and relatively unhappy matches playing for that very side. It followed that in the summer holidays of 1949 Colin was invited to play for Kent 2nd XI, making 35 for a solidly professional team against Norfolk at Norwich.

In Colin's final summer at Tonbridge, 1950, he showed that he was simply too good for his own age group. He scored 1,033 runs, averaging 79; a record which only Christopher, his son, has come close to beating. Originally Colin had intended staying at Tonbridge until 1951 when he would have been eighteen, the normal leaving age; but his father, who never had quite the same concern for his school work as for his cricket, thought he ought to leave that summer free for a shot at a full season in the first-class game.

So in Colin's final summer at Tonbridge, when he was also head boy, he dominated his opponents' bowling in a way that he was rarely able to do consistently again. There were times when Maurice Tate, the great Sussex bowler who had become Tonbridge's coach, forgot to signal when umpiring during a school match, so engrossed was he in Colin's stroke play. He even went so far as to compare Colin's on-driving to that of Bradman. Once, he told an opposition bowler that he was not going to give Colin out because 'I promised you at lunch that you are going to see some on-drives worthy of the Don, and he hasn't been in long enough yet.'

Again Colin scored a century against Lancing, as the previous year in the second match of the season; he took 175 off Christ's Hospital; an unbeaten century off Old Tonbridgians; six for 66 and 95 runs against Dulwich; another century, against Band of Brothers; 96 in a victory over Clifton at Lord's, his final innings for Tonbridge and one which took him to 1,000 runs for the term. In five years he had made 2,894 runs at an average of 40 and taken 216 wickets at thirteen runs apiece. These, of course, were exceptional figures for a schoolboy, even if Colin did feel that his bowling had not shown the improvement which might have been expected. He was to realise that it had regressed to the point where it would be of little use to him as a cricketer at a higher level. By his own admission it looked ordinary when he captained both the Southern Schools and the Public Schools at Lord's. He did, though, make another century, and a half-century. Having played for Kent's 2nd XI, Colin would not now join any other county. He had qualified by going to Tonbridge, a school which had probably nurtured more first-class cricketers than any other. Had he been educated at Marlborough, his father's initial choice, he would most likely have gone to Leicestershire or Surrey.

The call to play first-class cricket for Kent came earlier than anticipated. Their side of the early 1950s was, at best, a weak one, and during Colin's last summer term they had sought permission from Tonbridge for him to play against Leicestershire. It was refused. He had to wait until August for his opportunity. David Clark, the Kent captain, had said he wanted 'to break him in' during the last few matches of the season. At Derby, where he made his debut, he found himself isolated in the amateurs' dressing-room until Les Ames, who was leading the side in place of the injured Clark, eased Colin's discomfiture by moving in alongside him.

Colin's first meeting with Ames was a memorable one – or so the story goes. Bar his cap, which through superstition he always put on first, he was completely naked. It is a story which, according to Ames, is apocryphal. The reality, and it was a harsh one, was that in their first match together Ames was out for a pair. Colin fared a little better, making fifteen and 26, taking a catch at long-leg and the wicket of Pat Vaulkhard, lbw. He bowled twelve overs altogether in a match which Kent lost by an innings on a wet and uncovered pitch, and was not displeased with his performance. Apart from his isolation in the amateurs' dressing-room he was disconcerted only by the swing of Cliff Gladwin, a bouncer from Les Jackson and a giant pair of spectacles with which his team-mates greeted Ames after he had recorded a pair.

Colin played in three other matches, one of which was against the touring West Indians on a turning pitch, without conspicuous success. He scored 104 runs in seven innings in all, caught his catches and minded his p's and q's. All of which did nothing to deter him from his ambition of playing for England.

Colin left Tonbridge at the end of the Easter term of 1951 garlanded with honours after a year as head of school in addition to being captain of cricket and rugby, and having had four years in the racquets pair. Small wonder that he was sad to be leaving for Oxford. He left armed with a Heath Harrison exhibition, an award worth £60 a year that went to a student educated at certain public schools as specified by the benefactor himself. It was different from a Heath Harrison travelling scholarship in that it was given for academic excellence on the basis of an entrance examination. Sporting prowess was not a consideration. Nevertheless, in the 1950s sportsmen were valued: there was a commitment to excellence at games and it was apparent to the admissions tutors that Colin possessed precisely that. Twenty or 30 years on it would have been a different matter, hence the decline in cricketing standards at Oxbridge. Colin had even sat a scholarship: Tonbridge had given him a sound education and he was aware that sport was not everything. He would have liked to have read history, but settled instead for geography.

As for his summer of first-class cricket before going up to Oxford, it was a full one. Clark had promised to give him his chance and, if he did not succeed, he could fall back on 2nd XI cricket. Colin was chosen for what transpired to be Ames' last match for Kent – he slipped a disc and was unable to complete his innings against Nottinghamshire. And Colin, too, had his difficulties. He even asked to be dropped after not progressing beyond single figures in the first two matches, against Nottinghamshire and Hampshire, for whom Shackleton and Cannings had him out for four and a duck. Tom Crawford, another Old Tonbridgian who was leading Kent in place of Clark, refused his request, and his decision was justified when Colin made 27 and 47 in a low-scoring match against Northamptonshire. He ran into further form with a century for the Free Foresters against Oxford which led to an invitation to play in the festival at Scarborough under the eagle eye of Len Hutton, the England captain. There followed Colin's highest score for Kent that season, 90 against Hampshire and Shackleton, who had troubled him earlier in the season. He was learning already to play the percentages, to eschew risks. This was partly forced on him by circumstances: he was now batting at number four in a weak side and conscious that he had to contribute. That season Kent slumped to sixteenth position in the County championship.

Colin finished with 891 runs, 820 of them in seventeen championship matches at an average of 26. He became the youngest player to be capped by Kent after scoring 71 against the South Africans at the end of the season. Clark presented him with his cap in the president's tent, which *Wisden* reported, was 'fully merited'. Cowdrey was, it said, 'exceptionally mature in his approach to the game. He developed into the most reliable batsman in the side after Fagg.' He departed for the traditional annual Scarborough festival in good heart. He was to play for the Gentlemen against the Players, whose attack included Alec Bedser and Roy Tattersall, bowlers who bent their backs even in this kind of end-of-season jollity.

It was this match more than any other which brought his

name to the fore. Hutton was leading the Players and began to take notice of this extraordinarily mature cricketer who was only just out of school. He could hardly fail to do so since Colin scored a century, and yet it was not so much the weight of runs as the manner in which they were made which left an indelible impression on him. In build as well as technique he appeared to be a craftsman. Colin had had to bat on a damp pitch and ride his luck: he was dropped three times, the first chance given off the second ball he received. He had to battle, which would have impressed Hutton all the more. Hutton, the pre-eminent technician, was reminded of Walter Hammond. He advised Colin during his innings and commended him at the close, which impressed Colin enormously. This may have had something to do with Colin's tendency to express appreciation of excellence from the slips in later years; for the present he greatly admired Hutton, his approach, his technique and his elimination of faulty and reckless shots.

Even today, Hutton is probably unaware of the great influence he had on a cricketer who was as much a Novi in the first-class game as he had been once at Tonbridge. Hutton recalled, many years later, that it was Colin's temperament which initially impressed him so. 'He was gentle, never vicious, and it was that which reminded me of Hammond. He did not believe in inflicting punishment on the ball.' Hutton recognised his ability to see the ball early — 'and that is so important for top players'. It was, more than any other innings, the one which marked him out as a Test cricketer of the near future.

Chapter Three

International Impressions

F OR THE NEXT TWO years, Colin was not able to live up to the extraordinary impression he had made at Scarborough. In this he was not helped by playing in weak sides both for Oxford University and for Kent. Senior cricketers who had not seen his innings for the Gentlemen were sceptical of a reputation emanating from one match. In the three seasons Colin played for Oxford, from 1952–54, they did not win once, which puts into perspective their difficulties of more recent times.

Nevertheless, Oxford lost only once in those years to a Cambridge side which has never since been as strong. Colin enjoyed his cricket, even if he had played on sufficient true pitches not to benefit as much as others from the Parks. It was doubtful whether his game developed as quickly as it would have done had he continued to play for Kent throughout those summers. In his first year he was given his Blue after just three matches and made 92 and 54 against the Indians, but then struggled to score nine in an hour and a half against them for M.C.C. at Lord's. He was roundly barracked. At Canterbury he atoned through making his first hundred for Kent off the same opposition.

In the University match he made a half-century, which he improved upon in 1953 when, as Oxford's captain, he scored their first century against Cambridge for five years. Again he was compared to Hammond, this time by E.W. Swanton in the Daily Telegraph. Two strokes predominated in this innings, the off-drive and the forcing shot wide of mid-on. Poise and balance were much in evidence, wrote Swanton. He brought to mind a photograph of Colin when he was eighteen and playing a shot that was 'the very image of Hammond', the head still and the feet firmly planted. Timing was everything, and he was never hurried. Before the summer was out, Colin played

31

two other notable innings, both of them half-centuries, for the Gentlemen against the Australians at Lord's. It was against an attack that included Lindwall, Miller and Johnston.

For Kent, Colin had to contend with the difficulties that beset all struggling sides. There were consternations in his first years over the captaincy. Clark had stepped down to be replaced by Bill Murray Wood, a man whose best cricketing days were well behind him. And he did not endear himself to those whom he led. It was as a result of player power (again putting later years into perspective) that he was dismissed – in 1953 the entire Kent side, including Colin, indicated to the committee that they would not play for Kent again if Murray Wood captained them in another match. The committee had little alternative but to issue a statement, in the middle of Canterbury week, saying that he would be relieved of his post. Doug Wright, who was appointed his successor, then pulled a muscle, which meant that Colin took over the captaincy for Kent's next match against Leicestershire. He was 21 years old. On a crumbling pitch he was pleased with an innings of 81, his highest score for his county that season. As in 1952 he comfortably exceeded 1,000 runs in all cricket; he was only 83 short of reaching 2,000.

He was learning now how to build an innings. At school he was launched after a few sighters. At university and in County cricket he began to see that steering an innings was not only harder on account of the accuracy of the bowling, but that it was a science. He observed that leading batsmen would often start with a quick single while they became accustomed to the bowling and the pitch. Hobbs told him he would try to hit the first ball he received to the boundary and, as he was an opener, it would quite often be a loosener. The bowler would be stiff and, conceivably, nervous.

Colin, too, suffered from nerves at the beginning of an innings. Indeed, he was as nervous as anyone, and not merely when it was a major match or he was feeling out of sorts. He sometimes took guard twice by mistake. He saw this not as a weakness but as a help: if he was too relaxed he would be susceptible to playing a poor shot. He learned, too, from Bradman, who would walk slowly to the crease, giving himself time to adjust to the light. After a couple of overs Colin found that his focus became clearer and that his grip on the bat was more natural. He tried to keep his bottom hand as relaxed as possible. 'I used to work on the hope of a single from every over,' he wrote in an article in *The Young Cricketer*. 'The more a bowler is attacking, the more opportunities for stealing runs. The difficulties arise when the fielding side goes on the defensive.' It was a similar approach to that of Ken Barrington, with whom he played much of his Test cricket. Initially, they would both accumulate to long leg or third man. Colin would play a good length ball on his stumps as straight as possible, through the 'V' between mid-on and mid-off. An adventurous stroke which, say, a West Indian would be prone to try as soon as he went in, a flick through mid-wicket or a drive past cover point, was not for him. That was to be played only when he was on top of the bowling.

Limiting himself to four, or even three shots in his first half-hour at the crease meant, of course, that a moderate bowler could often dictate to him, an exceptional batsman. He of all batsmen had more than one shot at his disposal for each ball, yet he would be prepared to wait for an obvious bad delivery to score from. It meant, too, that the moment to turn defence into attack was not an easy one to choose. If the bowler was holding sway, this became problematical; for a lesser batsman it would have been a challenge he would most likely have lost. Colin was quite capable of surmounting this difficulty, but he had been coached that there was one particular stroke for every ball, and that left little room for improvisation. It was an approach born from days when limited-overs cricket and bonus points had no existence in anyone's imagination. He did, though, have a clear picture in his mind of the gaps in the field and when, as one contemporary put it, 'his mind was uncluttered', he had an unerring ability to find them. His drives would be so well timed that the ball would gather sufficient pace to elude the fielder giving chase and yet only trickle over the boundary. Complications arose when, as Ted Dexter suggested, he became confused because of his capability of playing more than one shot to any given ball. Dexter, a great theorist himself, said, 'It may be that his complicated thought process left him weighing up the two or three or even more possibilities so that he dallied while pondering alternatives.'

Colin was gifted enough to be able to select a shot before the ball was bowled – and bring it off. This, though, was reserved for dull draws when he was well established, and when the wicket-keeper put it to him that that was the way to liven up the match. He did it to amuse himself and others rather than to show off.

The game Colin grew up with was the one which suited him and, by and large, his method was effective. He was a cricketer for the 1950s rather than the 1980s. Because of the reputation he was building up, because he did not have any technical failings and few visible signs of nerves, opponents did not generally pressurise him at the start of an innings. Yorkshire were an exception, often planting a silly point as soon as he came in. Peter May saw this as 'taking advantage of his niceness'; in the north of England they saw it as a way of unsettling him. May said he would have tried to drive the fielder back, but that was not Colin's style. It would have been too crude, and he was too cautious to do other than look to collect his first runs in singles. He developed a habit of pushing forward with bat and pad together against all but the quickest bowling, an approach which was foiled if the opposition crowded him, seeking a catch off bat and pad. Colin's grouse when this occurred was that the fielder did not – could not – remain still, and in moving infringed the laws defining fair and unfair play. He was tempted to displace the fielder, as May would have tried to do, 'but when it came to it, courage has failed me and on reflection I do not regret that', he said.

Always a good listener, Colin assimilated technical knowledge. He was not one to relax after a match in the conventional way with a few drinks, although at Oxford he did go to Vincents, the sportsman's club. If he went to a pub bar, it was more to put in an appearance than to wind down. There are no lurid tales of him drinking or losing self-control: Charles Walford's admonishments had left no scope in him for the dilettante and, besides, his concentration on cricket was such as to preclude debauchery. For Colin, moderation was the ultimate virtue. At Oxford, when he was not at lectures he was playing cricket, and when he was not doing either he was ensconced in revision. Academic pressures, notably the Preliminary Examination in his first year, saw to that.

The summer of 1954 was Colin's last at Oxford. He made centuries against Kent and Sussex but again was unable to effect a victory. The University match was notable for a partnership of 180 in two hours between Colin and Mike Smith, another future England captain, who finished with a double century. That year Colin did not, in fact, bat as well as he had done in 1953, although he scored in excess of 1,000 runs for the fourth year in succession. For Kent, *Wisden* said, 'he rarely did himself justice with the bat'. He was sent a letter from M.C.C. asking if he would be available for the tour to Australia and New Zealand that winter but it did not concern him overmuch: he was one of 30 who had been sounded out. The party was to be announced in July at a time when Kent were playing Surrey at Blackheath.

A contest often dominated by Surrey went, on this occasion, to the very end. As Colin made for his car to leave the ground, he was startled to hear horns blaring and Kent members shouting at him. Their wirelesses had told them that Colin, not yet 22, was on the boat for Australia.

His initial reaction was more of embarrassment than elation: there were prominent Surrey players he had just passed in the dressing-room who had not been included, and he thought it best to scarper. He felt, at first, that he must have been Hutton's choice, yet it proved to be the influence of others who made up the captain's mind. Gubby Allen, then a selector, was the first to commend him. Allen's guiding principle in selection was, 'when in doubt go for class'. Ames was also influential. And the fact that he was so young counted in his favour rather than against him. That he had not scored a century in the County championship, had not been on tour and had not had an especially good season were overlooked in favour of his class. The very best cricketers are often in the England side at the age of 21, and Colin was thought to be among the very best.

There was but one Test remaining that summer, against Pakistan, for which Colin was made twelfth man and had to field for only twenty minutes before his inoculations for the imminent tour put him out of action for the rest of the match. His feeling was one of relief rather than regret: he was as nervous as he had been when he first played for Tonbridge at Lord's. But there was scant time to brood on it. After an enjoyable two-week Oxford tour of Denmark, which he had arranged before he learned of his selection, the ship left for Australia in mid-September.

Colin's parents came to Tilbury to see him off, and were immensely reassured by Hutton's demeanour. He told them he would take care of him, which was precisely what he did when, on arrival at their Perth hotel three weeks later, Colin discovered his father had died. Ernest's last act was to hear on the wireless news of Colin's first innings of the tour at Colombo. Only 54, he had died of heart trouble.

The upshot was that Colin became more self-sufficient, although from that moment on Hutton ensured he was not left alone to mope. For this, Colin was deeply grateful. There was no question of his returning home: the funeral would have been long over by the time he arrived back in England. Hutton had by now warmed to him as a person as well as a player: 'I always felt he was a bit shy and needed someone to push him. There were some similarities between him and Bob Wyatt – he was not too ambitious and was too easy-going. The difficulty he had was that later he did not have anybody to give him support.'

On the field, Colin had impressed Hutton in his first innings for M.C.C. on the tour. In the mid-voyage match at Colombo against Ceylon, he made an unbeaten 66. Near overwhelmed by the occasion and his own nerves, he found himself able to stroke the ball all round the ground in spite of being unaccustomed to the parched heat. Hutton included him in the side to play Western Australia, a sure sign that he was under consideration for the first Test. A score of 41 and, better still, a partnership of 125 with his captain helped Colin's cause immeasurably; he was to clinch his place with two centuries against New South Wales, batting, it was stated in a report, 'most brilliantly when brilliance was permissible'. He had to play circumspectly to ensure the match was saved. In the first innings he put on 163 with Hutton and, promoted to open in the second innings, ignored considerable barracking from the Hill. He made 110 and 103 in that match against the best opposition in Australia; only Denis Compton had previously scored two hundreds for M.C.C. or England in Australia. Thereafter Hutton saw Colin not just as a member of his Test side but as an opener. Again, it was his temperament that so impressed Hutton. Colin was not disputatious and was not prepared to argue, but, when he was out for four and a duck against Queensland in the last match before the first Test, going in first, Hutton changed his mind. 'I don't think you will be opening,' he said, and sidled away.

It was in Sydney that Colin had his first difficulty with the press, although it was indicative even then that he was becoming adept at mastering the art of giving interviews. An un-named author made him out to be a priggish youth who had just left school and who referred to 'my dear old schoolmaster'. Colin had the measure, though, of an interrogation about going out with girls (he was still a bachelor). 'What an extraordinary question,' he replied to the amusement of his colleagues. Like Richie Benaud, an opponent on this tour of a like age, he understood the workings of the media. He was especially impressed with the way Hutton handled press conferences. On this tour he formed a lasting friendship with John Woodcock of *The Times*, who with the commentator Brian Johnston and Michael Melford of the *Daily Telegraph*, all from similar backgrounds to Colin, became in turn godfathers to his younger children. And E.W. Swanton became a considerable ally.

At Adelaide Colin had his first meeting with Bradman. He and Peter May were invited to a dinner at his house. It was the beginning of another lasting friendship, one which extended beyond cricket to the golf course and the real tennis court, to which he was introduced by Colin. From then on The Don took a considerable interest in Colin's doings, starting in the first Test at Brisbane. Batting at number five, he made a creditable 40 in the first innings on going in at eleven for three. 'Rough time for a young fellow to come in. Good luck to you!' said Keith Miller, who proceeded to give him a vicious bouncer first ball. He was caught, he thought, off a boot rather than his bat after he had added 82 in a stand with Bailey which lasted more than two and a half hours. 'Cowdrey had done enough to prove his temperament for the big occasion,' wrote E.M. Wellings of the *Evening News*. 'Few had been in doubt about it previously but it was pleasant to have it confirmed at the first attempt and in the most testing conditions possible. It looked then as though he might become the outstanding young cricketer of the series. It also looked as though those of us who saw in him a future Test captain were not going to be disappointed. There was character both in him and his cricket.' He displayed his off-driving to good effect and was prepared to use his feet against Johnson's off-spin.

In the second innings, though, with England facing a heavy defeat, he fell back on defence. In 70 minutes he played just three scoring shots and was unwilling to venture out of his crease. He was ultimately out to a ball from Benaud which he intended to leave alone, but did not withdraw his bat from the line. The ball met it and deflected on to his stumps. The M.C.C. manager, Geoffrey Howard, remarked, 'In such cases the batsman seems able to imagine only one possible way of getting out – stumped. He forgets the many other ways.' It was negative batting but in the context of a defeat by an innings and 154 runs, seen as nothing more than that. There were bigger targets for the critics, notably Hutton for putting Australia in to bat.

In terms of statistics this was only a reasonable start. It was improved upon in the second Test at Sydney where in his second innings Colin made a half-century. Its significance was that in a low-scoring match he shared a match-winning partnership of 116 with May, the first of many times they mutually benefited from batting with each other in Test cricket. Colin alluded to their partnerships as if they were games of bridge, with May leading with an ace and his junior partner prepared to wait his turn. For three hours they were together until Colin's judgement and patience lapsed. Having made 54 he was tempted out of his crease by Benaud. Attempting to loft the ball over the sightscreen, he spooned it into deep mid-off's hands instead. It was an uncharacteristic error – and one he was rarely to repeat. Subsequently he played slow bowling mostly from the crease.

In this match his strokeplay was, if anything, more spectacular than that of his partner, who made a notable hundred. Colin's driving in front of the wicket was again the feature of his batting, the ball met with the full face of the bat. Arthur Fagg, his Kent colleague, had impressed upon him the need to move early at the crease against the quickest bowling and it was Hutton's influence which made him predominantly a front-foot player against pace. His driving evolved to an extent that by adjusting the point and angle of impact or by turning his wrists, he could send the ball wide of a fielder in the cover ring. It came naturally to him: years later he could not comprehend why Christopher, predominantly a leg-side player in a leg-side game, was struggling to drive balls of good length through the off-side. Colin was already an off-side player learning his art in what was fast becoming a leg-side game. The Australians by now would have worked out his methods, yet they found a batsman whose technique was sound enough for him to gather runs with relative ease on the leg-side as well. He became a completely adaptable batsman.

These were the qualities, enhanced by his temperament and maturity, which Colin possessed when, having just passed his 22nd birthday, he made the first of his 22 Test centuries. Many would claim it was his best. It came at Melbourne in the third Test of the series and was made against Lindwall and Miller in full cry. England were again struggling, at 21 for two and then 41 for four. The ball was kicking off a length and swinging considerably. Yet Colin was more surely behind the line than anyone else; again he was seeing the ball early. He appeared, outwardly at least, to be completely in command, nerveless and not lacking in concentration. Inwardly, he admitted, he was fraught with anxieties. It was a chanceless innings of 102, made out of 160 in three and three-quarter hours and out of 191 in all. It was as responsible as Tyson's bowling for determining the outcome of the Ashes – England won by 128 runs – and was applauded by the Australian crowd as they would have done had the century-maker been one of their own. Their generosity heightened Colin's thrill.

From that innings Colin's future as a Test cricketer was assured. No matter that he was out to an error of judgement, and not for the first time on the tour. Hutton was moved by his batting and could not get over the time with which he had to play in spite of the ball coming through the air more quickly in Australia than in England. If he had a criticism, it was over

Colin's ambition, or, rather, what he saw as a lack of it. This was the one difference he perceived when asked, as he was, to compare Colin with Hammond. 'Wally was hungrier – you could see it in the look on his face, whereas Colin always had some feeling for the bowlers,' said Hutton.

After that innings, Colin had much to live up to: he was judged by a different yardstick, even though, as he said, circumstances were constantly changing. He told Patrick Murphy for his book, *The Centurions*, 'At Melbourne everything went right – I had some luck and also played to my full capacity – but that was something people took for granted. I feel sorry for David Gower today: he has looked a class player since he was 21 at Test level, yet people expect him to turn in great innings irrespective of the quality of the bowlers and the wicket.' To illustrate just how much was expected of him, one need only turn to E.M. Wellings' account of the tour, *The Ashes retained*. He writes:'Cowdrey's first Test century confirmed him in the highest rank though with scope still for development, for it was clear he would climb far higher with experience. As yet Cowdrey was an inconsistent mover. For no good reason he was inclined on occasions to get himself into a strokeless groove, when his batting became pawky and apologetic. If that happened at the start of an innings the probable result was a small score, as happened in the second knock of this match. If it happened in the middle [of an innings] there was a fair chance that he would re-emerge and again become the real stroke-making Cowdrey. The truth of the matter was that Cowdrey had not yet persuaded himself that his natural, firm game was the best for all occasions.' Wellings did concede in the next paragraph that there was practically no other fault to be found in his batting.

Such criticism, from crowds as well as writers, did affect Colin. In the fourth Test at Adelaide, which England also won, Colin attempted to liven up a slow session with shots he had not previously tried in Test cricket. Hutton sent out England's twelfth man, Vic Wilson, with a couple of bananas to quell his appetite: Colin swiftly got the message. He finished with 79 in England's first innings, excelling with the cut more than any other stroke on this slow pitch. With Hutton he added 99 and with Compton 70, and batted in all for five

Colin's first tour. His pivotal hook off Benaud brings four runs at Adelaide in the fourth Test against Australia in 1955. He made 79. (The Times *photo library)*

hours. In the second innings he was out for four to Miller before England, needing just 94 to win, scrambled to victory with five wickets intact. Colin also had his nose broken in this match, when fielding in the gully. The ball leapt up at him from a crack in the ground and that, coupled with a chill, put him in hospital. It would have resulted in him missing the final Test at Sydney had it started on time.

That it did not was owing to much heavy rain. There was little purpose to the match once it was underway, England having retained the Ashes. Colin, not fully fit but playing at Hutton's insistence, was out without scoring in England's only innings. He was rarely seen in his best light when there was nothing at stake and the scoreboard read, as it did when he went in, 188 for two. His average came down to 35 for the series and 37 for the tour – but that was misleading since his

41

major innings were played in times of adversity, as they were throughout his career.

Hutton compared him with Hammond; some who were there compared him with the young Hutton, yet possessing additional strength. Colin could become, it was reckoned, an even greater batsman, as well as a future England captain. Hutton, who had taken a £1 bet with Gubby Allen before the tour that Vic Wilson would end it with a higher average than Colin, gladly paid up.

The tour wound on to New Zealand where Colin made a total of 64 runs in two completed innings in the two Tests, both of which England won. He flew home early to see his widowed mother, who was ill. That, coupled with financial difficulties (his family were of modest means) and a feeling that he would be achieving little by returning to Oxford, decided him upon his next course of action. It was one which would lead to his courting considerable controversy.

National service was, in 1955, still compulsory. At some stage Colin would have to undertake it, and stick with it, for two years. This would, of course, mean a major disruption of his cricket career. On arrival at the R.A.F. base the medical officer, on noting Colin's history of foot trouble, referred him to a specialist in London who examined and discharged him immediately. The R.A.F. had no wish to be saddled with paying Colin a pension for the rest of his life for causing permanent damage. His national service of two years lasted 26 days.

There were loopholes known to those who were intent on opting out of national service. Poor eyesight and compassionate reasons such as a single parent dependent on the son for income were two. Flat feet was a third, and it was the reason why Colin's case reached the House of Commons. Colin, outwardly fit and tanned, had had no difficulties with his running between the wickets or, indeed, his batting on hard surfaces in Australia. No sooner had he been released from national service than he ran into spectacular form, which was just about the worst thing he could have done. Gerald Nabarro, the Conservative M.P. for Kidderminster with the handlebar moustache, challenged the Minister for War, Christopher Soames. He told the House: 'There is really no excuse for Colin Cowdrey and the remainder being able to evade military service simply on the grounds, evidently, that they earn large sums in civil life or are prominent sportsmen.'

Soames was curt in his response. 'I must absolutely refute the inferences cast by you on the medical authorities,' he said. There was no option but to discharge a man 'when the medical advice is as definite and unequivocal as it was in the case you have in mind'. He said that in the nine years since the War, 928,000 national servicemen entered the Army. Of these, 11,000 were discharged in the first sixteen weeks of their service and only two were 'prominent people'. Colin by now belonged to that category and, since the matter was fully aired in the Press, his size eleven and a half feet with their troublesome toes brought him a bombardment of mail, some from cranks, some from parents whose sons were detained, forcibly, in the services. The letters pursued the same theme, that he was dodging the column, and they were still coming in twenty years later at a time when his feet continued to give him pain. One anonymous correspondent wrote regularly. Colin complained of neither that nor of his feet, although he thought at one point that his career would be ended prematurely.

All in all it was a trying period for Colin. In County cricket his form was prolific – he reached 1,000 runs that season playing in only fourteen matches – but because of his national service contretemps and a damaged finger took part in only one of the Tests against South Africa. It brought him a half-century and plenty of bruises from their tall fast bowlers, Adcock and Heine, whom he tried to combat – unsuccessfully – by playing off the front foot as he had done in Australia. He was gauging their length quickly; it was their height and bounce which troubled him. Subsequently he developed the facility to play off the back foot with equal ease. He managed to adapt, *Wisden* said, 'in the manner of the true masters'.

As early as when he was ten years old Colin had studied the movements of Hutton as to when he chose to play forward and when he opted to go on to the back foot. Only after half an hour he was more confused than he was at the outset, for reasons he discovered later. Colin learned in time that the great batsman could play forward or back at any time on a decent pitch. If the ball lifted when he was going forward, he could steer it through gully or short-leg. If it was a half-volley or full toss he could equally well dispatch it off the back foot. The key was balance and timing. He discussed this at length in his instructional book, *Tackle Cricket This Way*.

As a general rule, Colin believed in playing forward as often as possible. On the hard pitches in Australia, the maxim with the then lbw law was 'if in doubt, push out'. As was to be expected of one brought up with conventional coaching on true pitches, he was safe within a conventional framework. At the core of all his movements was perfect co-ordination. The secret to successful batting was, he felt, to keep his head still and to move towards the middle of the ball. If his head fell back or away, his timing went awry. When going through a bad patch, he would repair to the nets and relax his body and grip while keeping his head still and eye level.

Because Colin saw the ball early, had unimpaired concentration, could restrict his backlift and his shots against the quickest bowling, was an excellent runner between the wickets and, not least, because he was courageous, he was ideally suited to open. Both Hutton and May, who had taken over the England captaincy for the series against South Africa, thought him well equipped to do so. Hutton, in fact, regarded him as the best opener in the country in the mid-1950s. Quite why he developed an almost pathological hatred for it was a mystery to his colleagues, not least because it brought him a fair amount of success. Colin felt, though, that he was temperamentally unsuited to open and, although he was persuaded to do so on occasions throughout his career, he never changed that opinion. He would dread being out early and having no further part to play for the rest of the day. And there were times when, as captain of Kent, he was loathe to go in first for a run chase: he preferred to promote the sloggers. His evaluation of his own batting did not extend necessarily to thinking that he was best equipped to win the match. Also, having fielded at first or second slip throughout the opposition's innings – he soon became a specialist fielder – he liked to have a break before batting. His concentration was already drained.

After Hutton retired, there was – inevitably – a void in the England side. Hence the selectors asked Colin in 1956 to open the innings for Kent and duly picked him in that position for the entire series against Australia. He opened with Peter Richardson, whom he was to entice away from Worcestershire to join him in playing for Kent and who found him 'a marvellous runner between the wickets'. The highlights of their summer were putting on 151 at Trent Bridge and 174 at Old Trafford, the latter overshadowed by Jim Laker taking nineteen wickets in the match. Colin failed to make a century in the series, twice being out in the eighties and making just 244 runs in eight innings, which bore out his reservations. Yet opening for Kent he was prolific, making 1,000 runs in the County championship for the first time. It was as an opener that he was selected for M.C.C.'s winter tour of South Africa, a decision with which he concurred, reluctantly. After a moderate start this was reviewed and he went in down the order, Bailey partnering Richardson in each of the five Tests.

After his prodigious first tour of Australia, great things were now expected of Colin. Yet in spite of his restoration to the middle of the order he continued to have a struggle surmounting the difficulties caused by the pace of Adcock and Heine. Against the accurate off-spin of Tayfield he experimented with a lighter bat. He felt he had technical failings, even though others did not spot them. He made just one century in the drawn series and returned home disappointed despite having enjoyed the hospitality and beauty of the country. It was to be his only tour to the Republic.

He returned, moreover, with his Test place by no means secure. West Indies were touring England that summer of 1957 and, as he had done in 1950, Sonny Ramadhin proved mystifying in the extreme: not even the wicket-keeper knew which way he was going to turn the ball. In the first innings of the first Test at Edgbaston he bowled England out for 186, taking seven for 49 without extracting much spin. It was now that Colin's technical experimentations and adjustments were seen to good effect: although not able to pick the leg-break, he resolved that if he played forward early, the bat slightly behind his front pad, it would not matter. He would play Ramadhin as he would an off-spinner. If the ball turned into the bat, Colin reasoned that the umpire would not be able to give him out and if it was

For a bulky man, Colin had quick reactions: foiling Sobers at the Oval in 1957. Evans is keeping wicket, Trueman at short leg. (The Hulton-Deutsch Collection)

a leg-break, he would not be out anyway. He was unlikely to be caught at backward short-leg since his left pad was in the way. Because he was not playing with his bat in front of the pad, a ball ricocheting off both was liable to land in front of square. It was only when the lbw law was changed, so that a batsman could be given out to a ball pitched outside off-stump unless he attempted to play it, that Colin became more positive. Even then, he did not alter this mode of defensive technique to any great extent.

There was a drawback in this theory which May, his captain, realised could well be counter-productive. If the attack was not taken to the spinner, he, the spinner, would dominate. Colin preferred to play spin from the crease, although he did at times move out of it to appease the critics. He grew up, after all, in an era when it was accepted that a slow bowler should be combated with footwork. For Colin, not the quickest man on his feet anyway, the risk he took by so doing was as much losing his balance as losing his wicket. His game was based on being solidly positioned as he played a shot. 'His greatest anxiety was not nerving himself to play fast bowling but to go down the pitch to the spinners in the days when that was expected,' said Tony Pawson, his friend and Kent colleague. 'It was an ordeal for him.'

So Colin stayed in his ground, content to play second fiddle to May when they began to build a partnership in the second innings. He did so to the extent that it was a triumph, the greatest triumph, for his innate caution. The two of them came together, as they had done at Sydney three years earlier, knowing that only an exceptionally lengthy stand could bring England back into the match. They batted in partnership for eight hours and twenty minutes, adding 411 through intense strength of purpose. 'The concentration, the restraint, the technical excellence of these two innings could not be over-emphasised,' wrote E.W. Swanton. 'Never have two young cricketers built such a monument to patience and determination.' It was a Test record for the fourth wicket, the highest stand ever made for England and the third highest for any side in the history of Test cricket.

On this sluggish pitch Colin eschewed all risk, although when they had put on 250 and May urged him that caution was still necessary Colin struck three successive half-volleys from Ramadhin to the boundary. His pad play, left leg thrust to the pitch of the ball, demoralised the bowlers whose constant shouts for lbw came to naught. Ramadhin bowled 98 overs in that innings, more than any bowler had in an innings before (West Indies had unwisely omitted Valentine, their left-arm spinner).

May made 285 and Colin finished with 154, his highest Test score to date and the first Test century he had scored that was based on defensive batting. It included sixteen fours and 63 singles, and showed above all else that he had the stomach to compete at the highest level. He was to follow it with another large score, 152 at Lord's. This took him three hours less than his innings of 154. He added scores of 55, 68 and two, finishing the series averaging 72. In all cricket during the summer he made 1,917 runs, exactly the same total as in 1953. The difference now was that he was averaging 51 an innings as opposed to 43 then. Small wonder that these early years of his career were, to him, the most enjoyable.

Chapter Four

The Master Technician

I F CHARLES WALFORD exerted an exceptional influence over Colin's formative years, Stuart Chiesman, a similarly forceful character, gave him direction in adulthood. He was the antithesis of Colin: a hard-nosed self-made businessman who did not countenance fools, cared for committees only if he could chair them and was fond of telling and embellishing stories. A generous benefactor of Kent and Kent cricketers, he was held in some awe by Colin, who in 1956 became his son-in-law.

Chiesman and his brother, Russell, took over the eponymous family business from their father and uncle when it consisted of a small draper's shop in Lewisham. It became the large flagship departmental store of a group in Kent which, by the time of Stuart Chiesman's death in 1969, numbered seven in all. They tended to be sited near one of Kent's numerous first-class grounds so that Chiesman could indulge in his favourite occupation between the start and close of business on a Saturday. His favourite occupation, that was, after work.

He was a benefactor of charities, too, notably the Blind; a large draper's charity at Mill Hill, of which he was senior trustee; the Kent County Playing Fields Association and the Textile Benevolent Association, which endowed beds and wards in many convalescent homes; and he was to leave his sizeable house in Chislehurst, with its five acres of land, to Rochester diocese. Named Graham Chiesman House in memory of his son who was killed in a plane crash at the age of thirteen, it is still used as a retreat for youth groups.

There was an infectious enthusiasm about Chiesman which transmitted itself to those he met in the course of business or on Kent grounds. He saw its cricket club, when he became chairman in 1958, as an extension of his stores: he had no great knowledge of the game, which some of the players joked about. They appreciated, though, the interest he showed in them, especially those trying to make their way in the side.

49

He had a particular regard for Derek Underwood: Chiesman's chauffeur drove Underwood, who was highly enamoured with travelling by Rolls Royce, to Taunton for his first match. After taking 100 wickets in his first season at the age of eighteen in 1963, Underwood was given a cheque by Chiesman for £100. Chiesman also looked after the interests of the members and supporters, whom he would canvass for hours. He gave the club, during his chairmanship, 15,000 shares in his company, which was by now a public one, and a further 1,000 shares towards Kent's centenary appeal.

Altogether he lived life to the full, if not ostentatiously. He became High Sheriff of Kent, forged friendships with Sir Robert Menzies, the Australian Premier who became Warden of the Cinque Ports; and Harold Macmillan, then Prime Minister; and thought seriously about standing for Parliament himself. He settled for chairing the Chislehurst Conservative Association. He was a keen gardener, played water polo with Leslie Todd, the Kent cricketer, golf in the H.A.C. Cup at Chislehurst and bridge whenever he could spare the time, notably on holiday in Barbados each winter. He shrimped on the Kent coast, where he owned a second home, and watched Arsenal and Charlton play football. He did not believe in retirement; equally, he did not believe in bringing work home.

Chiesman was already on the Kent committee when Colin was introduced to him at the St. Lawrence ground, Canterbury, in 1955. There being no M.C.C. tour that winter, Kent wanted him to have some form of winter employment. Chiesman suggested he should work in the store at Lewisham, which he duly did, arriving in time for the autumn sales and becoming befuddled in the drapery department. Leslie Ames recalls the incongruous sight of Colin selling, or attempting to sell, towels behind a counter. Ames knew he was not cut out for it and Colin soon surmised much the same, not least because he wanted to spend his Saturday afternoons watching Charlton Athletic, of whom he was to become a director, at their nearby Valley ground. Chiesman wanted Colin to become a tougher businessman in his own image; but Colin was simply not the man for it. Hence their relationship was based on considerable respect for each other's gifts:

Stuart Chiesman, wearing a Band of Brothers tie. (Carol Keith)

they did not, for instance, become as close as Colin did to the Duke of Norfolk. It was soon apparent, as it was to Whitbreads and then Barclays Bank two decades later, that Colin's strengths in the commercial field lay in public relations. Ames always maintained Colin should have been an ambassador, such was the time and consideration he was prepared to spend, even at that young age, on fatuous queries from complete strangers. Alan Gibson, the writer and broadcaster, once referred to him in this light as 'the man who will go the extra mile'.

Chiesman, Colin's first employer, had been left a widower at the age of 27: a thrusting businessman with three small children. Graham, Penny and Ann were brought up by a succession of nannies and independent schools: the girls were sent to Ravenscroft School in Eastbourne, which subsequently

51

closed. Penny then went to Farringtons in Chislehurst. Extroverted and determined, she inherited her father's entrepreneurial streak. She was also fond of sport. Having been a competent runner at school, she became a qualified instructor with horses. She had been watching cricket at Canterbury for two years before she met Colin and genuinely enthused over the game: she named her dog after Doug Wright, the Kent and England leg-spinner. Ann, who was married shortly after her, remained linked to cricket, in a more tangential way. Her husband, Dr Richard Glover, was a contemporary of Peter May at Charterhouse and a sportsman; but one more consumed by boats than games on dry land.

Colin met Penny on the occasion when he first met her father, in 1955; and before the start of the 1956 season they were engaged. As with the majority of cricketers, the wedding had to wait until September, and even then there was time only for a two-week honeymoon in Cornwall before preparation for Colin's next tour, in this case to South Africa. They were married at the church of St. Nicholas, Chislehurst, by the Bishop of Rochester. Peter May was best man and David Sheppard, later to be a contender with Colin for the England captaincy, also officiated at the service.

Colin became a director of Chiesman's and was well remunerated: he was of particular value to the company in that he was a public figure, a recognisable face. That the business was concentrated within Kent only helped, as his image there was that of an unblemished cricketer. Thus Chiesman's were able to gain a form of advertising and promotion through publicity that was of immense value.

Hence both parties benefited. Chiesman was pleased to have an exceptional Kent cricketer as his son-in-law; for Colin, who did not always enjoy the best of fortune, this was a fortuitous marriage. It gave him financial independence and consequently independence from Kent C.C.C. In due course he was driving Jaguars (the number plate MCC 307 depicted his highest score, made in Australia on the 1962–63 tour), which he was prepared to lend to fellow players. He had his own secretary who accompanied him to grounds. Not least, his father-in-law was his Kent chairman for eleven of the fifteen years in which he led the county.

In 1957, when he became captain of Kent, Colin had reached maturity as both an individual and as a cricketer. He was only 24 during that summer and was of the opinion that an English batsman was not truly the master of his art until he reached the age of 30, a rather later age than his counterpart overseas; and yet Colin's development and technique were such that his prime lasted longer than most. It could be said to have stretched from 1957, by which time he could master pace and spin alike off front or back foot, to 1968, when he alternated attack with defence against West Indies in a magisterial way. In these years, arguably Gary Sobers alone middled the ball with such frequency.

'The fun of batting is the special target to achieve,' he said, and this was a simpler objective when Kent or England were on a winning streak. His batting was seen at its best when his captaincy blossomed, and vice-versa. The alchemy applied both ways.

'When he is in the mood I always feel that I want to measure his bat, because it seems so much broader than anyone else's and gives forth an especially melodious sound,' said Trevor Bailey. The flip side of this ability was that Colin was capable of edging the away-swinging ball more often than most. 'He was good enough to get a touch,' they would say, as if to imply that he was too classy for the bowler who had just dismissed him. So he learned to counter this by not following the ball, keeping the face of the bat closed and playing down the line of middle stump, not concerning himself if he was beaten. The mode of his dismissals in Test cricket was invariably caught: he would be dismissed thus roughly four times as often as he was bowled, and approximately six times as often as he was lbw. This pattern was similar in all his cricket. He was rarely stumped since he rarely ventured out of his crease; and infrequently run out since he was an excellent judge of a run and quicker between the wickets than his bulk would suggest.

It was perhaps because he was so good, because generally the bowler was not in his class, that he began to theorise to an inordinate extent. Some, like Don Bradman, would merely have decimated the bowling; others, like Barry Richards, would have become bored; but to Colin it was an intellectual exercise.

Few understood this; it was as if his batting was schizophrenic. 'Batting always fascinated me,' he said. 'Life becomes a bore if you've nothing left to prove, if you're not stretched. I relished the challenge of surviving at the wicket, of trying a few experiments.' Jim Laker, greatest of off-spinners, likened bowling at Colin to trying to get past a barn door. 'But,' he said, 'I did not mind bowling at him because I knew he would not try to hit me out of the attack.' Great and ordinary players alike thought he took technical experimentation too far, even if it was often confined to the nets. Leslie Ames could not comprehend the theorist in Colin, in particular the way he would experiment with his grip in the nets. 'That was something for lesser players, not when you have the finest technique anyone has ever had,' he said. At Oxford, Colin became taken with the batting of Mike Smith, who developed the ability to chip the ball over the inner ring of fielders. Colin suddenly decided to try to do likewise, even though everyone else, Smith included, would have given anything to be able to bat like Colin. Even May, his closest cricketing friend, once remarked to a colleague: 'How complicated can you get?' At Melbourne in 1966 Colin was caught at the wicket off Walters, having played a delightful innings of 79. He admitted that he was responsible for his dismissal: 'I knew as soon as he let go of the ball that I could have hit it past cover's left hand, but I thought I'd run it down through the slips instead.' He could not comprehend the amusement of his colleagues. It was an example of what Ted Dexter described as 'all his batting being a matter of pre-consideration, the thought process comfortably preceding the physical action. Colin's mind and body were tuned to a fine pitch in his search for the complete answer to every ball, every bowler and every situation.'

He wished to succeed or fail on his own terms. Alan Ross, the cricket writer, wrote that 'narcissistically he declined to disfigure his own reflection'. He did not believe in hitting himself into form. If the mood and timing were not syncronised, he would be becalmed. The orthodoxy and lack of violence in his character was reflected in his cricket and he was prepared to change neither at the crease.

This might explain why a county bowler of average talent

consistently pitching just short of a length and bowling to a defensive field could restrict him as well, if not better than a more experimental bowler of a greater standing. There was little fun for Colin in that kind of batting and he saw it as no test of technique. It was a base form of art, and one which held scant appeal. The nagging seam-up medium-pacer was the one bowler who could contain Colin for lengthy spells: yet when a particular Test bowler evolved a means of dismissing or restricting him, as Wes Hall and Richie Benaud did, Colin ultimately proved equal to it.

Seam bowling, which did not exist as such at the outset of Colin's career, predominated in county cricket from the 1960s onwards. Colin referred to it as 'the most significant technical development in post-war cricket,' and even thought that because of it, County cricket was sometimes a harder game to play in than Test cricket. There were two all-rounders in particular who were able to constrict Colin: Mike Taylor, who played for Nottinghamshire and then Hampshire, and Barry Wood, of Lancashire and, after Colin retired, Derbyshire. In particular, Colin hated facing Wood.

Such bowling would generally be accorded the epithet 'useful'. It was not of international standard. Yet, given the grassy, slow pitches which came into being in the 1960s, it would tax Colin more severely than better and quicker performers in the same conditions. As well as disliking it aesthetically and lamenting the demise of the spinner, Colin favoured a greater balance between bat and ball. 'There was so much more interest and fascination in trying to unravel the spinners' knot than there is in the medium-pace seamer.' He regrets still that he did not play more of his cricket against spinners.

Trevor Bailey cites two other reasons for Colin's relapses from greatness: his capacity for worrying and what he saw as his sunny nature, both of which were a handicap in a game played at first-class level for six days a week, with a Sunday game of one sort or another thrown in. Although Colin was fortunate in having to play little one-day cricket – at least by comparison with his sons – Bailey felt he suffered more than most from having to play too often. It was hard, when he had had a surfeit of cricket, to coax him into a recognition of his reserves of talent. Perhaps the key to the way he liked to play

lay in a comment he made once to Ted Dexter: 'It is easy to lose the thread,' he said, 'when you clip a leg-side half-volley for what inside you seems to be a certain four and it turns out to be a comfortable piece of fielding practice for mid-on. Then you do it again and wonder what has gone wrong with the system.' Colin enjoyed finding out.

Other than seam bowlers and those who allegedly threw, Colin was tested to the full when he was at his peak by two very disparate types, the volatile fast bowler in the form of Wes Hall, and the guileful leg-spinner, Richie Benaud. This was a test of technique as well as resolution. Hall regarded Colin as his 'bunny', and with Chester Watson subjected him to the most intimidatory bowling of the day, breaking his left arm in 1963. Benaud, by bowling leg-breaks around the wicket to a full length, pitching the ball on leg-stump, devised a way of tying him down before seam bowling came into vogue. Yet Colin found means of counteracting both, and built them into his technique.

When Colin went to the Caribbean as vice-captain to May in 1959–60, he was recognised as one of the foremost players of quick bowling in the world. 'It has been said that nobody really enjoys batting against very fast bowling which normally contains a goodly sprinkling of bouncers . . . . be that as it may, there is no doubt that Colin was a particularly fine player of pace,' wrote Bailey. Yet facing Hall and Watson, he not only came up against genuinely fast bowling but bowling that was testing the resolve of the umpires. Hall, Watson and Roy Gilchrist were the harbingers of those who took intimidatory measures to the extreme in the 1970s and 1980s, dismaying Colin at the end of his career and afterwards, when he assumed high office in the game.

After failures in the first two Tests, Colin was at a loss as to how to cope. 'I was beginning to wonder whether I had reached the end of the road,' he wrote in *M.C.C.* 'I had played an enormous amount of cricket but I could see nothing in my armoury to counter the staggering pace of Hall and Watson.' It hardly helped that May, as with Hutton, saw Colin as the ideal opener and, in his firm way, persuaded him that going in first was the right position for him; Colin was, quite simply, one of the best players of pace in M.C.C.'s party.

Repaying Hall: Colin swings a bouncer to the boundary at one of his favourite grounds, Sabina Park, in 1960. He made a century and 97. (Central Press Photos)

So Colin came up with the wherewithal to play it. In addition to restricting his movements at the crease, he would alter his guard against a bowler such as Hall, taking middle or middle and off rather than his customary leg-stump. There was a heightened danger here of an lbw decision against him, hence he had to ensure he did not play across the line of the ball. For protection against the bouncer he took to wearing padding as a chest protector, just as he did against Lillee and Thomson several years later. There was no suggestion then of donning a helmet or any other form of head gear and, besides, he would probably not have worn it. He felt, he said in retirement, that his movements would have been excessively hampered in a way that they were not by padding.

He took his padding, secreted beneath his shirt, into the third Test at Sabina Park, Kingston. Not for nothing has that proved to be one of his favourite grounds: in the first innings he made

57

114 and in the second 97, batting, he felt, about as well as he ever did. His century was largely a defensive innings – he struck only eleven fours – and in spite of his padding he was still badly bruised. He batted, or battled, for six and three-quarter hours. In the second innings he went for his drives and hooks in the knowledge that he had the defensive base from which he could counter-attack. Hall in particular maintained a healthy respect for Colin after that, rating him as highly as any English batsman he bowled against. It was neither Hall nor Watson who prevented Colin from reaching his second century of the match, but the relatively innocuous medium-paced Reg Scarlett, who had Colin caught at the wicket as he aimed to run the ball to third man. Others would have been dejected to have missed a second century by three runs; Colin was just pleased to have batted exceptionally well.

His batting on the remainder of the tour was equally memorable. He made centuries in the next two matches, a half-century in the fourth Test and another century in the fifth Test at Port-of-Spain. He finished with more than 1,000 runs on the tour, topping the averages. Still, though, he thought opening was not for him. 'I am one who by nature must get enjoyment from the game or else there is nothing. I can truthfully say the only times I have woken up in the morning and not joyfully anticipated the day ahead was when I was opening the innings in a Test match.'

Colin's confrontations with Hall and Watson's successor, Charlie Griffith, were to last throughout the 1960s amid raging controversies over whether Griffith did or did not throw. It was 1963 when England were next aligned against West Indies, this time in England. In the first Test of the series Hall removed Colin's leg-stump, his Caribbean guard of middle and off having left it exposed. It was one thing to be out to Hall; it was another to be bowled round his legs, as the press were not slow to point out. Colin had not taken into account the lower bounce on English pitches. He made four and twelve in that match, and four in the first innings of the second Test at Lord's. In the second innings his performance is remembered for a quite different reason. Had he scored a double or triple hundred it would not have had quite the same impact.

England had been left needing 234 to win. When Colin came to the crease, batting at number five, they were 31 for three. Again Hall was in devastating form, pitching constantly short of a length and striking Colin and his partner, Ken Barrington, all over their bodies. This in light which was giving way to gloaming. At the pavilion end, from where Hall was bowling, there were no sightscreens: the ball emerged from murky windows or the reddish hue of the venerable building. Colin had made a troubled nineteen when he involuntarily jabbed his left arm up in front of his face to ward off another short, kicking ball. Instinctively, he knew his arm was broken and that he would take no further part – or so he thought – in the series. Hall vividly recalls the agony on Colin's face: 'What really hurt me was the look in his eye as he was helped off. I was sure he was going to cry. He was in considerable pain, but it was not that which bothered him as much as the fact that he could not go on. Colin was convinced he could win the game for England and cursed himself for not spotting the extra kick in the ball.'

No-one admired Colin more than Hall for being prepared to return to the wicket at the death, when the match was splendidly poised. Brian Close, defending and then counter-attacking with similar courage, made 70 and set up a remarkable finish. When Hall began the last over, eight runs were needed, England having two wickets remaining. Singles came off the second and third balls and Shackleton was run out off the fourth. West Indies thought then that they had the match won: they could see no prospect of Colin returning, nor was there any intimation that this might happen. Suddenly, to a capacious roar, Colin emerged from the sub-fusc of the pavilion, left arm in plaster, struggling through the photographers. He went to the non-striker's end with two balls remaining and six runs wanted. Hall was determined not to bowl a no-ball; David Allen was intent on not taking any chances. He played out the over defensively with a calmness that belied the tension. If Colin had had to face up, he would have done so by turning around and batting left-handed to protect his arm. In due course the break healed; but he did not play again that season and it was a while before he was batting against fast bowling with something approaching his old confidence.

*Showing Christopher the rudiments of batting. Colin and holiday-makers at Lumley beach, Sierra Leone, in 1960. He said it was the finest beach he had ever seen – and the best pitch he had ever played on. (*The Times *photo library)*

West Indies were, for much of the period when Colin was at his peak, the strongest side in the world. There was a passion and ferment about their cricket which no other country could match at the time. No side with Sobers in it would play stereotyped, defensive cricket for long, if at all. Yet for Colin, nothing could compare with competing against Australia, for the bond between the two countries, the connotation of the Ashes and the inherent traditions set such series apart.

Overall, Colin had greater success against Australia in Australia than he did in England. Of his five full tours, the only one on which he did not excel was that under Illingworth in 1970–71—and for reasons that most probably had more to do with his frame of mind than any inexplicable loss of ability. He especially enjoyed his cricket under May, even if on the 1958–59 tour of Australia England were soundly beaten. Colin made a century on that visit, 100 not out in the third Test, but made only one other large score, 84, in the series. His average of 43 runs an innings was repeated exactly on his next tour there, in 1962–63, under Dexter, and give a run, it was his career average in Test cricket. The price he paid for playing against Australia more than any other country was a lower overall Test average, for he did not manage anything like the same success against them in England. It is significant that in *The Incomparable Game* he lists Tyson and Hall as the fastest bowlers he faced and Gilchrist as the most awkward, but Lindwall as the most skilful. Later he amended this: he found Lillee and Thomson the most fearsome of them all.

He thought highly, too, of Lindwall's new-ball partner, Miller, and from 1958–59, Benaud. Newly installed as Australia's captain, Benaud had become an extremely competent leg-break and googly bowler of expansive variations. Colin had encountered him on his first tour of Australia and had been out to him more than once; but both then and on the 1956 tour of England Benaud was still learning his trade.

Benaud devised a method of containing Colin. The most shrewd of cricketers, he knew that Colin liked to play slow bowling from the crease, with liberal use of his left pad. He reasoned that leg-breaks pitching outside leg-stump would tie Colin down, and so it proved. For Colin, at that stage of his career, was not prepared to shovel the ball away. Not until the advent of one-day cricket did he attempt to clout the ball without inhibition. He preferred to caress the spinner. He also disliked attempting a conventional sweep shot because, he felt, it was not worth the risk. So he invented something which became known as 'the paddle'. Used against Benaud, it was effectively a tap to long leg. It eliminated the risk of a top edge, was played finer of the wicket than the sweep and thus would elude orthodox field placings. It was a shot propelled from an upright position rather than on one knee, hence allowing Colin greater balance. Even so, it was a more awkward shot to bring off against the leg-spinner than the off-break bowler since the ball was turning across the bat; yet it was effective enough for Basil

D'Oliveira to copy it, successfully, later in the decade. Colin was proud of his invention: he had proved, he felt, that he was not merely an off-side batsman.

Yet the summer of 1961, when Colin implemented this shot against Benaud, was in all probability the most disappointing home series of his entire career. Not only was he frustrated at not having made certain of succeeding May as captain of England, but his batting repeatedly failed him. In eight Test innings he amassed just 168 runs; he missed the fourth Test, the one in which Australia retained the Ashes, owing to illness. He did not, in fact, make a century for England against Australia in England until 1968. Yet it was a different matter playing against them for Kent. In 1961 he made centuries in each innings against the Australians, becoming the first Kent player to do so. This remains one of his proudest achievements.

Facts and figures, as Colin would be the first to observe, do not illuminate the entire picture. There is a difference between facing the new ball and highly charged fast bowlers on the first morning at, say, Kingston, than there is come mid-afternoon when the shine and zip have gone. It was not details in *Wisden*, Colin once tellingly remarked, that he would take with him into old age; rather, it was memories of those he played with and against. Had he been consumed by statistics he would clearly have achieved more, perhaps 200 centuries, as Ames suggested he should have made. But then, nothing irritated him more than comments to the effect that, 'if only he had realised how good he could have been. . . .'

It was in the 1960s that players and critics alike began to level this criticism at him, and it stuck. Not surprisingly Colin grew tired of it, not least because he had no apparent answer to how and why the great caresser of the ball should descend from the heights to become just another batsman. *The World of Cricket*, which by the 1960s was the most comprehensive work on the history of the game, re-iterated a familiar point – 'He cannot believe that he is a far greater player than most of the bowlers he faces and too often he lets them dictate to him when he should be dictating to them. Had he done full justice to his natural gifts he must by now have ranked with the greatest bats ever.' Yet cricket writers of the time rarely concerned themselves with analytical insights into complex characters.

By and large, they concentrated on the reporting of matches and evoking his good and bad days: 'A dolphin among minnows'. . . . 'Gambolling between the green and the blue as if cares were not invented'. . . . 'At his less good he seemed imprisoned by some interior gaoler, feet chained, arms pinioned, shuffling away a long sentence.'

There was no doubting that Colin was sensitive to criticism of his batting and all too aware, with the coming of television, of the proliferation of the media. He tried to fulfil their expectations, which, so far as his batting was concerned, were considerable. After making 113 and an unbeaten 58 against Australia at Melbourne in 1962–63 he said in response to John Woodcock's congratulations and comment that he must be relieved it was all over, the match won: 'Yes, but now there's the next one to worry about.' Other than when he made his first Test hundred in 1954–55, he could hardly have batted better in Australia than he had on that occasion. It was on that 1962–63 tour, in terms of statistics the most successful of all his tours there, that he made his highest score, 307, against South Australia at Adelaide. It was the highest score made for any English touring team. He averaged 57 on that visit under Dexter, who felt that Colin was at the peak of his career.

There cannot have been a more popular cricketer ever to visit Australia. If he was not playing, he was preaching by invitation (touring for him was a religious as well as cricketing crusade) and if he was not preaching, he was coaching or talking about cricket at schools. He enjoyed telling stories against himself, notably of his partnerships with Hutton. Once, when they had been through a particularly torrid spell from Lindwall and Miller, Hutton said to him: 'I don't know why you're doing this, Colin, you're not even being paid for it!' On another occasion, when Colin was playing and missing, he went down the pitch to Hutton and said, 'It's doing a bit.' 'Watching you play,' the captain retorted, 'you would be better off at home pushing a pencil.' Colin delighted audiences with his mimicking. He gave them a fair impersonation of Hutton. He was not averse to some mimicking during Test matches, particularly if the cricket was becoming monotonous. He would imitate the old amateur captains – Lord Hawke with his stomach hanging out – Graveney's grip on the bat, Compton's waddle and

Laker's finger inspection. Raman Subba Row recalls opening the batting with him in a Test and having a joke on the way to the crease as to whether they were attempting to win the match or to entertain the public. Colin was a leg-puller with old and young, colleagues and critics; and usually he did not mind having his own leg pulled.

Australian crowds empathised with him. But their players did not. Some of them could not take what they saw as inconsistencies in his attitude to walking. Colin was an avowed walker at a time when the majority of players absolved their responsibilities. Australian cricketers preferred the attitude of a batsman such as Bill Lawry, who stayed at the crease until given out. That way they looked upon good and indifferent umpiring decisions cancelling each other out. Bobby Simpson, Norman O'Neill and Neil Hawke, all prominent cricketers of the 1960s, criticised Colin for seemingly expecting the umpires to place their trust in him. Simpson claimed that Colin should pay the umpire the compliment of looking at him when a strong appeal was made, which, he said, happened on two particular occasions. The Australians felt he was out each time. O'Neill stated that 'when Colin receives a bad decision he tends to show it more than anyone and that annoys us. At Brisbane in 1958–59, at Melbourne in the same series and at Adelaide four years later he gave the clearest impression he was dissatisfied with the umpire's decision.' And yet, O'Neill said, there were times when he walked when he wouldn't have been given out. 'It seems to me Colin himself sets out to walk whenever he thinks he is out and so when he receives a bad decision, he tends to query it. He reacts as though the umpire should always know.' Hawke said that because Colin was an avowed walker, any dismissal which he queried would cast doubt in the minds of journalists and spectators. 'His method could be used to advantage if he chose to remain over a close decision and walk for the obvious. On an occasion when he was given not out, when he directed the ball into the hands of Wally Grout, he coloured noticeably and next day, addressing a church gathering, used the theme, "Are sportsmen what they were?"'

In between touring Australia under Dexter and then Smith, there was a series against them in England in 1964. It was a high-scoring one, although Colin, afflicted by injury, missed the Test at Old Trafford in which 1,271 runs were scored for the loss of eighteen wickets. His one score of note came at the Oval, an unbeaten and exciting 93 in a match that was affected by the weather. If, as a batsman, he was best remembered at the time for returning to the fray against Hall the previous year, as a fielder he became renowned for enabling Fred Trueman to gain his 300th Test wicket, also at the Oval. It was a highly-charged day, with Trueman taking his 298th and 299th wickets in the last over before lunch. The latter, that of McKenzie, had been caught by Colin. No-one on the ground missed the resumption of the over, but there was to be no hat-trick. In due course, though, Hawke edged Trueman to Colin at first slip, the ball travelling fast and to his right. Two famous well-used photographs tell of the incident, one illustrating Colin's excellent reflexes and the other depicting the ecstatic bowler giving Colin a mighty bear hug.

Colin was among the most reliable of slip fielders. It was logical that he should develop into a specialist since he saw the ball early, had a safe pair of hands and reacted quickly. His girth did not impair those reactions: he was surprisingly agile. It was on his first tour to Australia that he gained a reputation as a slip fielder, standing alongside Hutton and, since he was not fleet of foot nor possessed an exceptional arm, there he stayed. If at first slip, he concentrated on watching the seam of the ball as it left the bowler's hand. At second slip he concentrated on the edge of the bat and fastening his eye on the bounce of the ball. Always, he remained crouched and alert until the batsman had completed his stroke. Not for him any resting of his hands upon his knees. He was constantly mindful of how hard it was for a top-class cricketer to combine concentration with relaxation, citing that most slip catches were missed at an early stage of the innings. To this end, he did not when captaining object to fielders close to the wicket putting their hands in their pockets on cold days – but only when the bowler was returning to his mark.

Once established as a first- or second-slip fielder, Colin would rarely be stationed anywhere else, even at third slip or gully. As a captain, slip was the ideal vantage point. Only towards the end of his career, when Illingworth had to move him elsewhere

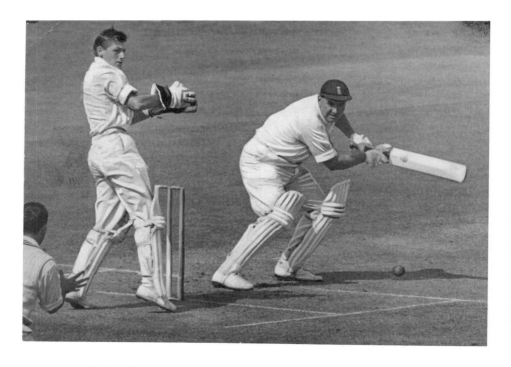

Colin's late cut, executed against the 1965 New Zealanders at Lord's. Ward is keeping wicket. (Sport and General)

on account of uncharacteristic lapses on the 1970–71 tour of Australia, or when the opposition's innings was reaching its climax in limited-overs cricket, was he hampered by advancing age and lack of mobility. Then he would finish up by the square-leg umpire or mid-wicket. When leading Kent, he reasoned that in the closing overs of a one-day innings the best fielders, or at least those with the strongest arms, should be positioned on the boundary, which would leave room for him to move to the inner field.

In Test cricket virtually all of his 120 catches (a world record until Greg Chappell broke it) were taken in the slips; and Colin stands comparison with Bobby Simpson and Phil Sharpe as the best of his generation. The disadvantage of fielding there, as we have seen, was that his concentration was spent by the time he was due to open the innings, if so required; the fun in it was to pouch a catch and pocket the ball while all eyes, the batsman's included, were looking towards the boundary.

If the description 'automatic selection' is ever valid or justified, it should have applied to Colin. And yet in the mid-1960s, when theoretically he was at the height of his powers, England omitted him twice. On one occasion the opposition was Australia in 1964 when, in spite of having a productive season for Kent, he had limited success in the three Test matches in which he played. The other occasion was against West Indies in 1966, when he lost the captaincy. Both times the decisions were taken on account of his lack of runs, although the selectors would have weighed his class against his current form. There was no knowing when Colin would suddenly find his touch since many of his finest innings were born from an indifferent sequence of scores.

In the interim, 1965, Colin had one of his most impressive summers, taking a century apiece off New Zealand and a strong South African side. He has spoken of how batting for him became pointless as an exercise in churning out runs against opponents unable to mount a technical challenge; yet invariably he scored heavily against the weaker countries: New Zealand, India and, before they became a strong cricketing nation, Pakistan. His four highest innings in Test cricket were 182 and 159 against the 1962 Pakistanis; 160 off the equally limited 1959 Indians; and 155 against the 1960 South Africans in the final Test, when England had long since clinched the series and he had the measure of Adcock. He constantly scored runs against New Zealand, averaging 146 from four innings against them in 1962–63, the highest he achieved in any Test series. The fun of batting, the target he set himself, was seemingly not discounted by playing sub-standard Test opposition.

Quite how much fun it was then to return to County cricket and enthuse about the game on a wet day before a handful of pensioners and dogs at Gravesend when Kent were not winning anything, was another matter. It may or may not be significant that Colin ended his career with a higher batting average for England (44.06) than for Kent (42.01). If he played too much cricket, at least it did not dampen his enthusiasm for long. For cricket held him in thrall. Although he missed numerous matches for Kent through Test calls, illness, injury and feeling the strains of playing in a Test, did not make many truly big scores in County cricket and by no means always scored 1,000 championship runs a season, it was an anomaly if he did not strike a rich vein of form at some juncture.

One of his leanest seasons for Kent, 1966, was not surprisingly one of his most trying ones for England. In 1964, when he had been dropped, his form overall was not affected. In 1966, though, his batting fell away, conceivably because he had had the England captaincy to contend with in addition. After making 69 in the first Test when playing under Smith, he made just one further decent score in the series, 96. Yet then to make out a case that he was a more successful batsman when unencumbered with the captaincy would be to fly in the face of his achievements in West Indies in 1967–68. It was the first occasion on which he had led M.C.C. for a full tour and who is to say that, had it happened before, both batting and captaincy would not have prospered in tandem?

In West Indies Colin's batting was a joy. He seemed to make a big score virtually every time he went to the crease. In the first Test he put England on their way to a large total with an efficient innings of 72. He made centuries in the second Test at Kingston, holding the first innings together for nearly six hours, and in the fourth Test at Port-of-Spain, making a dominating 148 in five hours. His 71 in 76 minutes in the second innings won the match and with it the series. Alan Knott called it 'the best attacking innings I ever saw him play. He just plundered the bowling.' He judged the scoring rate perfectly against the clock. In the final Test he did more than anyone to stave off a West Indies victory, his 'shrewd, commanding innings of 82' as *Wisden* called it, taking up much of the last day while wickets fell about him. This was masterful defensive cricket, just as in Trinidad he had batted in a more trenchant manner than some present had seen hitherto. He was particularly effective on this tour at flicking Gibbs and any bowler of medium-pace over mid-wicket with minimal arm movement, closing the face of the bat by rolling the wrists. He showed, too, that he had vanquished any unease he may have felt against fast bowling in the wake of his injury from Hall. Not once in this most rewarding of series for Colin did Hall capture his wicket. Hall was not quite the bowler he had been in the past; having lost a yard of pace he was unable to counter Colin's pivotal hook shot. Alan Knott, then on his first major tour, was fascinated by Colin's 'flair for analysis' and the way Colin made full use of his body weight. 'Batsmen who generate their incredible power from vigorous use of the arms and shoulders such as Gary Sobers and Ted Dexter frequently drive straight. But Colin, relying more on the pace of the ball to help him rarely does that, for he lets it come on to him before driving more square,' he said. 'He had probably become a more consistent batsman, though from all accounts he was usually not so exciting to watch as he was in his early days.'

His position as a middle-order batsman, to say nothing of his captaincy, was as secure now as it had ever been. So was his stock among fellow cricketers. It was a surprise when England lost the first Test of the 1968 series against Australia, in which Colin was twice out cheaply. In the second Test at Lord's, a match England most likely would have won had it not rained heavily, he scored 45 in their only innings. There was ground to make up at Edgbaston in the third Test.

He had an additional special reason for wanting to excel. It was to be his 100th Test match, a landmark reached by no other cricketer. 'It is one which he will pass without thinking for one moment that a bottle of champagne is called for,' wrote John Woodcock. 'He is too unassuming and abstemious for that.' The match was marred by bad weather and injuries to both captains and finished in a tame draw. Yet nothing could dim Colin's personal performance. Cheered all the way to the wicket, he made his 21st century in Test cricket and his first against Australia in England.

Australia's attack centred round McKenzie, who cramped Colin with the ball that cut back into him – once he should have been caught at the wicket – but no other bowler troubled him. He joined Hammond in reaching 7,000 Test runs. Even when he pulled a muscle in the back of his left leg and had Geoff Boycott, of all uncertain runners, to call for him, the ball still pierced the gaps. At the close of play on the second day he was five runs short. The injury stiffened, restricting

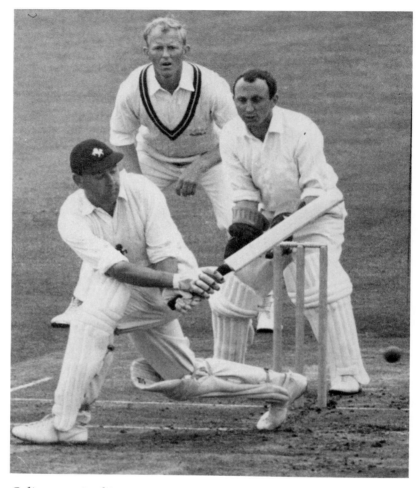

Colin executing his more conventional sweep against Surrey. Long keeps wicket, Storey is at first slip. (Central Press Photos)

his movements still further, and it took him 19 balls to go from 99 to 100, Boycott finally charging off on the coveted single.

The match petered out; and Colin was not fit enough to include himself in the fourth Test. His personal contribution in the fifth Test was more in terms of captaincy rather than runs, of which he made 51 in his two innings. Of considerably greater significance was England's victory, as a result of which they levelled the series; and D'Oliveira's century, which led to wider repercussions.

M.C.C.'s tour of South Africa having been cancelled, a short tour of Pakistan was formulated for early in 1969. It was spoiled and ultimately also abandoned owing to political turmoil, but not before Colin had made a dogged century in the first Test at Lahore to a background of cacophonous noise. The pitch, in fact, was the safest place on the ground.

Back in England, Colin began the 1969 season in excellent form. His eyesight, enthusiasm and finesse remained unimpaired. In his 37th year he was physically fit. In spite of carrying excess weight for much of his career, he had been given scant trouble by his knees, the bane of many a sportsman's life. His left arm had been broken but generally, although he had suffered numerous bouts of enfeebling illness, his injuries had been too few to be worth numbering.

In 1969 the John Player Sunday League was a novelty and, even though he was opposed to it in principle on religious grounds and found difficulty in looking upon it as anything more than an extension of Rothman's Cavaliers cricket, there was little reason why he should not prosper as those half his years would do. And he appreciated the financial benefits which would accrue for the good of the game.

Come May 25, Kent were leading the League table and their match against Glamorgan at Maidstone was televised. Colin swiftly compiled 39 before, as he shaped to play a forcing shot, he slipped on the wet surface. The crack when Colin's achilles tendon in his left foot snapped could be heard on television. He underwent an operation, recuperating through bicycle rides round country lanes, and was unable to play again that season, although in August he did make one appearance – against the all-England ladies team. 'I thought it would be the most charitable way of starting again,' he said. 'There have been odd moments this summer when I've contemplated giving up but I honestly can't think of life without cricket. I can't dream of retiring while I've got so much more to do.'

But after that he was never the same batsman at Test level, although he continued to bat consistently for Kent. This had little to do with the injury – he made a full recovery – but had much to do with losing the England captaincy. When he next played for England it was under Illingworth, against the Rest of the World in 1970. The series is not generally recognised now as having been official Test cricket but it was competitive enough at the time. Omitted from the first match through lack of form, Colin was included in the second match and contributed an innings of 64 to an England victory, thus, ironically, helping Illingworth to retain the captaincy for M.C.C.'s winter tour of Australia and New Zealand. He made two further decent scores in the series, 71 at Edgbaston in the following match and 73 at the Oval against an attack that included Sobers, Procter, Gibbs and Intikhab Alam.

Colin's tour of Australia that winter under Illingworth was the most dismal of his career. In three Tests he made only 82 runs and he was to play only one major innings before finding some solace in New Zealand, a century against Victoria at Melbourne which *Wisden* described as 'tediously slow and marked by wasteful running.' It took Colin more than five hours. *Wisden* is normally reticent in its match reporting, but on this occasion virtually accused Colin of losing the match. Although his was the highest score, 'his hesitant batting led to a collapse' – and Victoria won comfortably.

That was at the start of the tour. He made a half-century against a Queensland Country XI, 28 in the first Test, 40 and one in the second Test, struggled to reach a half-century against South Australia when opening and captaining, and was dropped for the fourth Test, the third in the series having been abandoned. By the fifth Test, isolated from the rest of the party in that he preferred to go his own way off the field, it was clear that his differences with Illingworth could not be resolved. And try as he doubtless did, his game would not improve. Recalled for the fifth Test in place of the injured Fletcher, he made 13 and dropped five slip catches. He was left out of the last two Tests. Only when he reached New Zealand, where he was warmly received, did Colin find some form. Omitted from the first Test, he made 54 and 45 in the second, batting with a certainty of stroke that he had not shown hitherto on the tour. It gave him heart for the English summer ahead.

Colin began the 1971 season in fine form, as did Kent. Thus he was selected for the first Test against Pakistan; but he made only sixteen and 34 and was dropped when Boycott was fit to return for the second Test. Colin took no further part in the series and had little further cricket that summer. At the end of June he went down with pneumonia severe enough for him to have to go into special care at hospital. It was assumed then that his Test career was over. He would be 40 the following year, Illingworth would not be pushing for his selection and younger players were coming into the England side. As he was relinquishing the Kent captaincy as well, it appeared as if Colin was nearing his swan-song. He, though, had other ideas.

Chapter Five

The Bane of Captaincy

C APTAINCY WAS, IN many respects, the bane of Colin's career. It brought him unhappiness, discord, ill-luck, criticism and only a moderate degree of success. At times, it also affected his batting. In the 1960s he became enveloped in countless debates and controversies as he was constantly looked upon as the second-in-command, the captain who could be relied upon in emergency. This was not, he said, an amusing or gratifying experience.

In 1957 he had taken on the captaincy of Kent. He was young but already an experienced cricketer, had the support of his father-in-law on the committee and subsequently as chairman, and no-one expected him to achieve instant success. There was no competition for the post, which he inherited from Doug Wright. It was a straightforward appointment: he was an amateur, had led Tonbridge and Oxford and was an established Test cricketer. He was able to formulate a long-term plan for success with Leslie Ames, whom he brought in as, first, manager and then secretary-manager. Although it was ten years before the first trophy was won, there was no suggestion that he should be dismissed, as might have been the case a decade later. It meant effectively that Colin could continue captaining Kent until he realised his ambition of winning the county championship.

In Ames, Colin recruited wisely. Experienced and fair, he was respected by players and committeemen alike. Captain and manager reckoned then that it would be the 1970s before they turned Kent into a champion county, and so it proved. In retrospect Colin felt his captaincy did not mature until the end of the 1960s, since prior to that Kent had not looked likely to win either the championship or the Gillette Cup. He was only 24 when he became captain and although his first sides included several individuals who either played for England or came close to so doing – Evans, Richardson, Brown, Ridgway,

*Colin's wedding to Penelope Chiesman in September 1956: May (right)
was best man, Richardson and Tyson were ushers. (Kemsley Newspapers)*

Prideaux, Wilson – Kent did not come within range of a trophy
until the next generation of cricketers had matured. By contrast,
Peter May hardly knew what it was like not to lead a winning
side and it was partly because he gained success with Surrey
at a young age that he retired early. Colin kept going until the
championship was his in an era when captaincy was something
of a duty. As Ames said to him on one occasion when he was
demurring over the prospect of becoming England captain, 'If
you're offered it, you must accept.'

For the most part, at least when free from controversy
and speculation, Colin enjoyed the art of captaincy. Had he
possessed, like May, county bowling of infinite variety, he
might well have become more aggressive and assertive. As it
was, he became a defensive captain of Kent, one who could
swiftly lose faith in a bowler whose line and length strayed.

This explained why for him, a tactician of innate caution, Derek Underwood was the consummate cricketer. He could always be relied upon. Before Underwood joined Kent and raised their expectations immeasurably, Colin was apt to become slightly bored if a championship match was heading ineluctably to a draw.

Tactically Colin knew the game as well as anyone. He was meticulous at field placings. He knew how to keep the opposition interested in a run chase. Yet his indecisive nature made it hard for him to effect positive decisions. He was known on occasion to escape from a technical challenge by absolving his responsibilities and nipping off the field; once a couple of wickets fell he would be back on. This attitude could extend to the pursuit of quick runs when, losing confidence in himself, he was wont to go in down the order. It applied notably in one-day cricket, since the coaching he had received from a young age left scant room for improvisation. His lack of belief in his own batting, coupled with his modesty, could extend to telling a lesser player that he would give him as much of the strike as possible. Once, Ames locked the dressing-room door to ensure he had to go in; no-one else could get to their pads. He remained the amateur captain in the sense that his vice-captain occasionally received a call from him from, say, Meopham police station. He was running late and could his deputy toss up for him and decide whether or not to bat? Ames would joke to Kent players about Colin telephoning him at the end of more than one hard-fought Test match to say that he was carrying some form of injury and would not be fit for Kent's match the following day. Neither was he enamoured with playing at Leicester or Headingley if it would mean having to toss up and converse with Illingworth and Brian Close and, as a southerner, receive cat-calls. He was not amused when Illingworth once belittled him by walking out to bat before he had led Kent on to the field.

Colin needed to be reassured that he was a great player, although it embarrassed him to know it. Yet it was the cricketers he captained, many of whom could hardly be mentioned in the same breath, whose need of reassurance was the greater. They could see for themselves just how good Colin was. Young players found Colin, who was trying to do the right thing by everybody and win each player over, asking them what he should do upon winning the toss.

His strengths as captain of Kent, particularly when in the 1960s they began to unearth young players of potential, were in essence an extension of his greatest strength as an individual: his consideration for others. E.W. Swanton said that he had never known anyone who cared more for other people's feelings. Underwood cites the presentation of his county cap by Colin during Kent's match with the Australians in 1964; Colin had telephoned his parents the night before. 'It might be worth your while coming to the ground tomorrow,' he told them. For Underwood's 21st birthday, celebrated during Tunbridge Wells week, Penny baked him a cake. Underwood never felt he knew Colin well, 'but there was an aura about him, and I was not the only one who thought that'. Colin would think nothing of collecting players from their homes, chauffeuring them around the country and taking them home again. And later, he would always visit the groundsman at Tonbridge when, as a parent or governor, he watched cricket there. Few cricketers can have given so much of their time to supporters, schools, good causes, even the church. Whether it was a player who came up to him in the pavilion or a supporter who ventured up to him in the street, he was always approachable. Colin, Chiesman and Ames were a formidable trio when it came to promoting Kent: indeed, Colin spent as much time with committeemen and members as he did in the dressing-room. His presence was always felt. 'He genuinely does not want to hurt people,' said David Kemp. Basil D'Oliveira said of him after the traumas they went through together, 'He is the gentleman of cricket.'

Colin was a paternalistic captain who was at his best when looking after young players. In the 1960s there was an emphasis on building up a family club, on playing attacking cricket and reacting to supporters. Kent maintained close links with cricket clubs within the county and many were the functions Colin attended to glean more about the roots of the game. He would not go to the pub after a day's play, unless he needed to put in an appearance. Instead, he would gather his players together for dinner or split them into groups. This was before team dinners came into vogue. Golf days were run so that new players could be integrated. He and Penny were especially kind to Kent's overseas players, John Shepherd and Asif Iqbal – and, later, Bernard Julien. Shepherd and Asif were shrewd signings by Colin, as indeed Julien was, although he never fulfilled his talents. Although always slightly aloof, Colin made an especial effort to impart information to the junior players, particularly concerning the way to bat on different pitches. They had few opportunities then of going abroad to play or coach in the winter, unless selected for their country. They learned as well, of course, simply by watching Colin bat. At the crease he would attempt to resolve any difficulties his partner might be having, rather than attempt to pinch the strike from him. It was then that his theory of adjustment of grip against fast bowling could be daunting for a younger and lesser player. His analysis, though, would be sound. To a batsman struggling to bisect the cover ring, as the young Mike Denness was once in Colin's presence at Folkestone, he would advocate a guard of middle and leg rather than middle. Consequently the ball would be played late and the field split. Bob Woolmer, who first played for Kent under Colin's captaincy, cites the many hours of help he gave him when travelling to and from matches. Woolmer was to model his game on Colin to an inordinate extent.

The future of the game was always uppermost in his mind, as, for instance, when Kent played a touring side. The spirit of the occasion was of greater importance than Kent winning the match. When Ted Dexter once made a double century against Kent, Colin, it was clear, regarded him as a breed of cricketer to be protected rather than merely as an opponent (which is not to say he did not want to get him out). This admiration, though, was a complex affair: it extended to the point that on another occasion, when Sussex were poised to beat Kent on the last day of a championship match at Hastings, Colin, who had batted, did not appear on the ground. The embarrassment of losing to Dexter was, apparently, more than he could bear. In the event Kent saved the match.

But despite Colin's kindness and consideration, the majority of players he captained at county level – and, later, for England – hardly knew him as a person. They admired his batting but were confused as to his constant theorising, his shortage of confidence in himself and his lack of conviction as both a person and a captain. His sensitivity towards others meant that he could not always bring himself to tell a player he had been dropped, and there were those who learned on the car radio that they were not on a forthcoming tour. On occasion, notably with Ken Higgs in the Caribbean, this led to a major row. Younger players were confused, too, by what they saw as his ambivalence over walking. Those who played for Kent in the early 1960s preferred to be led by Peter Richardson, who deputised for Cowdrey, and this did not go down well with Colin. To return to the county game after the rigid discipline of Test cricket was hard for any cricketer: it was harder still for Colin, who had to collect the threads of captaincy after regularly missing county matches for each of the fifteen years he led Kent.

On the premise that a captain is only as good as his team, Colin was best served by both county and country at the end of the 1960s. Having achieved his ambition of winning the championship in 1970, he gave up the captaincy when Kent had as good a team as any in their history. His legacy as England captain was also a winning XI, having beaten West Indies and almost regained the Ashes, achievements which have sometimes been overlooked in the writings of his contemporaries. Of these, the most damning comments came from Ray Illingworth and Mike Brearley, who were generally recognised as exceptional leaders. In his book, *Captaincy*, Illingworth wrote that Colin 'rarely built warm, lasting relationships with his team because of a tendency to have favourites. He was condemned to ultimate failure as a captain through essentially being an amateur trying to make himself a professional.' He did, though, feel that Colin became more assertive as he grew older. Brearley, writing in *The Art of Captaincy*, noted that Colin possessed many of the attributes needed by a good captain. 'He was intelligent, charming and had generosity. But he was not a good captain because his problem was himself; he lacked decisiveness and was too concerned about how things (and he) looked.'

Questioned closely by Barry Davies on BBC TV's 'Maestro', Colin confessed that he was perplexed by Brearley's comments. 'I shall have to go away and think about them,' he said, which hardly suited Davies or those who made the programme. When young, Colin had seemed at prep and public school to be an accomplished captain. When relatively old, he was a decisive spearhead of M.C.C. and I.C.C. In the interim, few regarded him as a natural leader.

Colin's first experiences of captaining England owed everything to one factor, the recurring ill-health of May. Thus he was, inadvertently, saddled for three years with the tag of a stand-in leader. There was no question of his being able to usurp the authority and position of his friend, even if he had wanted to do so, for May, the country's premier batsman, was regarded as its rightful captain. It was in 1959, Colin's third season leading a lowly Kent side, that May became seriously ill. Colin was made captain for the fourth Test of a series against India so one-sided that the fun had gone out of it: even though this may have been a marked and, to many, a welcome contrast from struggles in County cricket, it was not to Colin's taste. And in his very first Test as captain he became embroiled in controversy.

His concern in that Test against India was, as ever, over how the game should be played. In this, the fourth match of the series, England were leading three-nil. In *Time for Reflection*, Colin wrote: 'Throughout Thursday and Friday I had felt very unhappy that there was so little interest being taken in the match. This attitude, though understandable perhaps, seemed a little discourteous to our visitors. All that Saturday's crowd and television viewers had to look forward to was a follow-on and a defensive grind by India. The whole prospect was as flat as a pancake. At that time the calls for livelier cricket were ringing out even louder than usual and during the evening I wondered how on earth anything could be done to enliven the match.' He chose not to enforce the follow-on in view of the settled weather and the holiday season and stated publicly that this was his plan if, as was likely, he had the choice.

In a less paternalistic age, Colin might well have been charged with condescension; as it was there was a hullabaloo about Test cricket becoming farcical. Colin had the tacit support of the chairman of selectors, Gubby Allen, and England won that match and the final Test; but his captaincy had not begun on a propitious note.

When Colin first captained England abroad, for two Tests on M.C.C.'s 1959–60 tour of West Indies, he was again deputising for May. A pattern emerged. He then deputised for Ted Dexter. Next, for Mike Smith. Then, effectively for Brian Close after he had been sacked. And finally, for him the unkindest cut of all, for Ray Illingworth. There was one overriding reason why selectors did not want him to be captain: his indecision.

The adversity which afflicted, even pursued, Colin throughout his career was evident on that tour of West Indies. Having been vice-captain to May on M.C.C.'s previous tour, to Australia in 1958–59, he was clearly seen as a prospective England captain. M.C.C.'s manager now was Walter Robins, who in that role and as an administrator was determined to implement the same brand of attractive cricket which he had promoted when playing for Middlesex and England. The eager antagonism that was his hallmark as a player was carried over into management. And he was not an admirer of Colin's conservative captaincy.

Colin took over the leadership from May, who was again ill, for the last two Tests of the series. England, contrary to expectation, were winning; Colin opted to sit on the lead. He did so by drawing both matches, in which he made personal contributions with the bat; but Robins was not to be appeased. He gave Colin a dressing-down for his tactics and thereafter the two did not hit it off. The facts were these: at Georgetown in the fourth Test England ensured they would not lose the series, and yet slow cricket on a lifeless pitch did not endear Colin to Robins. In the fifth Test at Port-of-Spain, where conditions again were not assisting the bowlers, it was debatable whether England might have won had Colin declared earlier. Instead, to Robins' chagrin, he refused to give West Indies the slightest chance of drawing the series, delaying his declaration until after lunch on the last day. West Indies were set 406 to win at 140 an hour on a pitch taking spin. They had lost five wickets by the time the match petered out. It was Colin's misfortune that no sooner had May retired than Robins became chairman of selectors. Only on one occasion in the years of his chairmanship, 1962–64, did Colin captain England.

He did lead them in 1960 against South Africa whilst May recuperated, and what was more he won an uneventful series. Colin, as in the Caribbean, was criticised for England's defensive cricket. In the fourth Test, when three-nil ahead, he

Colin edges Benaud past Simpson at slip and Grout behind the wicket during the 1961 M.C.C. match against the Australians. He captained England twice during the summer. (Sport and General)

did not deem it worth setting South Africa a run chase. He asked them to score 185 in one and three-quarter hours, which held no interest for them. That the cricket was uneventful was because the cricket on the whole tour was played out under a cloud: even in 1960 ructions over apartheid meant that it was suggested the tour be called off. Then there was controversy over the action of Griffin, the fast bowler; poor weather; and, most significantly of all, the fact that South Africa were outplayed. Their summer was over by the end of the third Test and, even though they managed to draw the final two Tests, they had scant luck. Colin won the toss in each of the five Tests.

Meanwhile Colin remained merely the caretaker captain, appointed one step at a time, and he assumed, as did everybody else, that May, once fit, would resume the captaincy. May was no great age and any thoughts of retirement he was keeping to himself. Still not fully fit in 1961, he asked to be omitted from the start of the series against Australia. Again Colin, on his own admission an inassertive captain when deputising for his friend, was appointed. The first Test was drawn, the second lost ingloriously. As against India two years earlier, Colin's deliberations were swayed by what he saw as a need to play entertaining cricket.

May's rehabilitation had taken the form of playing under Colin at Lord's; for the third Test he resumed the captaincy (the selectors voting three to one in his favour) with Colin's support. Free from his trials Colin's batting flourished. His innings of 93 in the third Test, and the inspired bowling of Fred Trueman, enabled May to win the match, even if England lost the series.

With hindsight, Colin felt that 'at Lord's I should have clinched the captaincy for years to come'. In *M.C.C.*, he wrote that had England won that match, 'I might have begun a long reign of leadership and so avoided the many rumpuses and embarrassments of the next few years.' Had May not returned to the captaincy, that might conceivably have happened. May was to play no further Test cricket after 1961 but his 'conscientious vice-captain' as he called Colin, was not given the opportunity to succeed him. 'I wonder,' wrote Trevor Bailey in *The Greatest of my Time*, 'whether Colin's Christian philosophy has not made him prepared to accept situations without complaint that many simply would not have tolerated.'

That winter, Colin having chosen to drop out of M.C.C.'s tour to India and Pakistan (then of little importance compared to playing Australia and West Indies) Dexter succeeded May. When Robins, the advocate of brighter cricket, was appointed chairman of selectors the following season, the more flamboyant Dexter retained the captaincy for the series in England against Pakistan. In addition to this, the spectre of May hung over English cricket: not everyone accepted he had retired for good.

For the real prize, the captaincy of M.C.C. for the 1962–63 tour of Australia, there were several contenders. May was not one of them. Dexter was the man in possession; the Reverend David Sheppard had been urged to come out of retirement by Robins, the idea being that if he re-discovered how to bat, he should be appointed; a third contender was Mike Smith; and, of course, there was Colin himself. Colin led England in the third Test that summer and was then chosen to captain the Gentlemen in their annual match against the Players (the last, as it transpired). Immediately beforehand, however, Colin was taken ill, went to hospital and did not play again for three weeks.

It became a two-horse race, with Dexter winning and Sheppard selected as a batsman. Colin, who understandably had expected to succeed May, was to be vice-captain again. The selectors were banking on his loyalty, since the prime requirement was for a cricketer who could run the side adequately in the captain's absence. Colin was capable of doing just that, without taking offence if his plans were countermanded by the captain. Vice-captains are often chosen with an eye to the future: in Colin's case he seemed always to be installed for the present, with the selectors seemingly never envisaging him as the successor. Both Dexter and Smith were younger than him.

It said much for Colin's love of the game that he was prepared to journey to Australia as vice-captain so often seemingly without complaint. Once, though, vexed that he would not be made captain, he dropped out of the 1964–65 M.C.C. tour to South Africa. Ostensibly it was for family reasons. But he had realised that Smith would be chosen ahead of him, Dexter having relinquished the captaincy in order to stand for Parliament. Certainly Brearley's theory applied to Colin as it did to Smith in 1964–65: that every time a captain is appointed it is either because there is no-one better or the man who apparently is more able has spoiled his copybook or is unavailable. For the next few years the England captaincy continued to be given to Colin and taken away from him in a manner described by John Arlott as 'pettifogging if it happened in a school or club'. Although doubtless he would have been a more contented man had he determined to concentrate solely on his batting, he saw the captaincy of M.C.C. to Australia as one of the greatest honours the game could bestow, conceivably the greatest. The call was not forthcoming in 1965 when Smith led England against New Zealand and South Africa and was then appointed captain to Australia. Once more Colin was to be vice-captain. He admired Smith's captaincy in the drawn series, had a decent tour with the bat and returned to England to start the 1966 series against West Indies under, he assumed, Smith.

However, Smith lasted but one Test, in which England were crushed. With doubts over his ability to play pace, the selectors turned once more to Colin, not least because he was worthy of a place in the side as a batsman. It was unlikely that any England captain would have won that series, and Colin was no exception. He was, at one stage in the match, close to beating West Indies in the second Test at Lord's. The recall of Graveney proved an excellent move, his resplendent 96 the first of several fine innings that summer. England had their opponents in substantial trouble, five wickets down in their second innings with only a minimal lead, whereupon Gary Sobers, the nonpareil, was joined by his cousin, David Holford, and England could not part them. Their unbroken stand of 274 ranks as one of the finest ever. Indeed, Sobers believes he played his greatest innings that day. Colin's tactics towards him were generally defensive, and they certainly were on this occasion: by pushing the field back he reckoned to entice him into going for his shots and, with luck, mis-hitting. Only now the mis-hits were not forthcoming. Those shots that were mis-hit simply did not go to hand. Mostly, the ball was sent screaming to the boundary. The critics panned Colin for his defensive tactics and Sobers wrote later that he was too cautious a captain; yet such was Sobers' brilliance that criticism had to be tempered.

In the next two Tests England were outclassed. They were beaten by a considerably better side; but a change of captaincy was still inevitable. Colin did not retain his place as a player, either; for he had not had a particularly successful series with the bat. As if that was not bad enough, his Test cricket that summer ended on an especially unpleasant note. West Indies having won the fourth Test at Headingley and with it the series, he went into the opposition's dressing-room to congratulate their players individually and collectively. He was immediately shunned by Charlie Griffith, for reasons explained later in *Chucked Around*: 'I refused to be patted on the back by Cowdrey since he had been at the wicket with Tom Graveney when the latter spoke to [umpire] Charles Elliott about me and as captain did nothing, in my opinion, to rebuke Graveney. I was therefore in no mood to be receptive to his congratulatory remarks.' Graveney had insinuated that the ball had been thrown. Then, when Colin went to his Jaguar to leave the ground, he found it had been extensively scratched and the tyres let down.

There were few people then who thought that Colin would ever again captain England. Colin himself could not envisage it. Besides, he was now 35 and would have to excel to win his place back as a player. Brian Close, who had achieved a memorable victory in the last Test against West Indies, was seemingly destined to remain as captain for some while to come.

Colin, tired of polemics, hoped to be left to concentrate on his own game and on captaining Kent, who were by now on the brink of winning the championship for the first time since he became their captain. There was no overseas tour in the winter of 1966 and the following summer Close continued as England captain, beating India and Pakistan with some ease. Colin was duly recalled, but not until the fifth Test of the summer. It was between that and the final Test against Pakistan that Close allowed his own judgement to become clouded in a county match between Yorkshire and Warwickshire. The day before the final Test began he was summoned to a disciplinary hearing at Lord's to explain alleged time-wasting tactics and, what was of greater concern, apparently striking a spectator as he came off the field. In 100 minutes Yorkshire bowled 24 overs, Warwickshire falling nine runs short of victory. It prompted another agitation, namely that if he were to become involved in a similar incident during M.C.C.'s tour of West Indies that winter, it could easily lead to violence on one of the more volatile islands.

On the day after the Test it was announced that Colin, and not Close, would be leading the M.C.C. party. The selectors, who had wanted Close, were overruled by M.C.C., with the result that they resurrected Colin. Worse, this was all made public when Doug Insole, the chairman of the selectors, admitted that Close had been their first choice.

So, thirteen years after he first toured with M.C.C., Colin had at last been chosen as their captain overseas. On the face of it, this was his most daunting assignment. For once, though, luck was with him. For a start, Ames was his manager – appointed before Close's fall from grace. While others on the selection panel had wavered over the merits of Colin and Mike Smith, Ames' influence had been decisive in Colin's becoming captain. The party went not so much as underdogs as completely written off: Ames was in a minority, possibly of one, in thinking that West Indies were not quite the side they were. He felt especially that Hall and possibly Griffith – 'although still a bit nasty' – were not the formidable bowlers of 1963 and 1966.

In spite of the disadvantageous position in which he had been placed by the muddle over his appointment, Colin felt now that he had grown into the captaincy. He had, after all, been leading Kent for ten years and had won his first trophy during the summer, the Gillette Cup. He had several months to plan his tactics which, as ever, were cautious ones, designed to frustrate the West Indian stroke-makers on their own true pitches. 'He was very deliberate and calculated,' Basil D'Oliveira recalled. 'He just held on and waited for the breaks. The idea was to frustrate Sobers so he became sick and tired of us, and that ultimately was what happened.'

The difference now in Colin's captaincy was that he had greater security of tenure. May, Dexter, Smith and Close would not captain England again. Tom Graveney said that, 'when he held the captaincy without looking over his shoulder, precious little criticism could be mounted against him. No unbiased judge could possibly fail to put Cowdrey ahead of Sobers in all the accepted arts of captaincy in that series.' Others reckoned that he had become hardened by criticism and was uncompromising, determined to make his critics eat their words. Ames, though, felt he was no tougher than before; his indecisive nature would still emerge. He would say at a team selection meeting, 'let's sleep on it for 24 hours', and would ring Ames in his hotel room the next day – to discover that Ames had not changed his opinion.

The series, and Colin's luck, was to turn in Trinidad, where the one positive result came about through Sobers, attempting to break the deadlock, being over-generous in his declaration. As for the major difficulties Colin had to surmount, this time they were not so much Sobers' own cricket, or Griffith's action, or even West Indies' excellence. Rather, Colin's mettle was tested by sub-standard umpiring and unruly crowds; and his natural diplomacy suited him to handle both admirably.

It was during the second Test in Jamaica, the most explosive of all the West Indian islands, that the rioting occurred. The first Test had been drawn and England, largely through Colin's century and some magnificent fast bowling by John Snow, were winning comfortably. Half the West Indies side were out for 204 in their second innings when Basil Butcher queried a catch at the wicket. It was the signal for the crowd, in their pent-up disappointment at the way they were batting, to rain bottles on to the ground. The players did not leave the middle as Colin walked to the boundary in an attempt to plead with the most unruly section and to diffuse the trouble. As he dodged the flying debris, appealing in vain amid the commotion for the match to continue, the police took the view that tear gas was needed to quell the rioters. Helmeted policemen with shields and truncheons had already formed a ring around the ground and Colin's actions had, if anything, exacerbated a highly awkward situation. Nevertheless, he was praised. 'He moved around looking more icy than I have ever seen before,' wrote Griffith. 'He was not playing the diplomat. He was a captain pursuing a trail of victory.' The tear gas dispersed the rioters – and some of the more staid members of the crowd as well. Half a mile away a meeting of the Jamaican Cabinet was disrupted. Play restarted 75 minutes later with the lost time to be added on to the scheduled playing time if necessary. It was.

Colin had agreed to this suggestion by the Jamaican cricket officials in the event of rain spoiling the final day. Yet it was not England who needed the extra time but West Indies. Sobers, as he had done at Lord's two years earlier, again batted superbly to save the match. His unbeaten century enabled West Indies to declare, leaving England 159 to win. They claimed the extra 75 minutes and, on a pitch fast breaking up, had them 68 for eight when play finally ended. In every way, the zest had gone out of England's game.

There followed the tragic boating accident to Fred Titmus in Barbados. He was forced to return home having lost four toes, his career seemingly over. After that and another high-scoring draw in Bridgetown, M.C.C. moved to Port-of-Spain and, unquestionably, Colin's greatest triumph as England captain. It was another high-scoring match and one which, like the previous encounters, appeared to be heading for a draw. England were 112 runs behind West Indies on first innings, Colin making his second century of the series. They had been troubled to an extent by the leg-breaks of Willie Rodriguez — although this was not evident from his figures — and of an unlikely figure, Butcher. It was this, plus the impression that England were weary, as well as sheer cussedness on Sobers' part that led to him declaring, challenging England to score 215 in two and three-quarter hours. A gambler at heart, he was bored with the stalemate — and frustrated with England, whose over-rate had slipped to eleven an hour. Close, who had transferred from pitch to press box (his advice was sought several times by Colin) and who had been pilloried for not dissimilar sluggish tactics, reckoned that was the only time he had seen Sobers truly upset.

It was a gambler's throw, for Hall had been dropped, Griffith was injured and Sobers was entirely reliant on himself, his leg-spinners and the indefatigable Lance Gibbs. Colin, for his part, was highly cautious, as it was his nature to be: he was concerned because he and other batsmen were having difficulty reading Rodriguez. The ball was obviously going to turn and even in the absence of Hall and Griffith, who would take an interminable time bowling their overs, it was a sizeable asking rate. Initially, Colin was markedly reluctant to go for the runs. 'We can't lose this one,' he said.

The consensus, though, was that Sobers had not done his sums properly. Ames, Graveney and Barrington, the senior members of the party, urged Colin to have a go. 'We would never have had a better opportunity,' said Ames, who himself had been frustrated that England had not won one of the first three Tests. Colin then led the way to victory in partnership with Boycott, his batting as thrustful as anyone present had seen from him. He made 71, England won by seven wickets with three minutes to spare and Sobers, whose sportsmanship Colin greatly admired, was criticised in a way that hitherto was entirely unknown to him. Colin was merely booed by the Trinidadian crowd. 'His offences,' wrote *Wisden*, 'were to have played two superb innings and to have led England much more skilfully than Sobers had led West Indies.'

The fifth Test in Guyana was a thrilling affair, England just managing to draw the match with nine wickets down in their second innings. It was now that Colin's mastery of slow bowling was seen to good effect, scores of 59 and 82 contributing as much as Boycott's century and Snow's ten wickets to England's cause. So Colin, discounted as a captain before the tour, returned to London with the Wisden Trophy to show to his growing family, his standing in the game higher than ever. Cricketers generally appreciated his enthusiasm for a life in which he had known his setbacks but had persevered while others had retired before their time. He had stated before the tour, rather mournfully, that he felt he had finished 'third in an egg and spoon race' when ultimately the selectors had turned to him. He had shown as well that there was a difference between captaining England at home and abroad. For the first time he had had his own command and although he remained the same innately wary captain who hedged against taking risks and who tended to believe that every player shared his own standards of responsibility, he was now leading with authority.

The focal point of Colin's cricket in 1968 was, as we have seen, his hundred in his hundredth Test. Yet even that was put into perspective by the D'Oliveira affair when the England party came to be chosen for South Africa, scheduled for the winter. That Colin did not regain the Ashes was an obvious disappointment, but his task, after England had omitted three bowlers from fourteen players and lost the first Test by 159 runs, was invariably a hard one. The intention behind taking an excessively large body of players to Old Trafford had been to further the team spirit that had been fostered in West Indies. The effect, though, along with an injury to Barrington, was to complicate England's selection. Bad weather then deprived England of a victory in the second Test, in which they dismissed Australia for 78, their lowest score for more than 30 years. Needing 273 to avert an innings defeat, they had lost four wickets for 127 when a much-interrupted match ended. There was some joy for Colin: he took three slip catches and so passed Hammond's record of 110 in Test cricket.

The third Test was also left drawn, England having the better of another rain-affected encounter, and injury deprived Colin of a place at Headingley for the fourth Test. He had not recovered from pulling a muscle severely in compiling his hundredth hundred at Edgbaston. By now Bill Lawry, the Australian captain intent on retaining the Ashes, was content to sit on his lead and avoid defeat. To that end, all went well for them until the last day of the fifth and final Test. They looked beaten when five wickets down and still well in arrears of England, but, just before lunch, a storm flooded the ground. Within half an hour the Oval was under water. The sun re-appeared at 2.15, prompting Colin, squelching out to the middle with trousers rolled up, to join the groundsman and volunteers from the crowd in mopping-up. By 4.45 play had recommenced, yet only 75 minutes remained for England, with all the side crowding the bat, to take the remaining five wickets. They did so with six minutes to spare, Colin switching his bowling until D'Oliveira made the crucial breakthrough, and then bringing back Underwood to account for the tail on the drying pitch. Colin and Underwood justifiably took the plaudits before their efforts were cruelly overshadowed by the eruption over the non-selection of D'Oliveira shortly afterwards.

Part two of Colin's five-year plan, as he called it, was now formed. This did not include a series against Pakistan, since one was not scheduled until 1971. Even if it had been, he would probably not have deemed it worth part of an ambition which extended only to matches against the major Test-playing nations. A short tour there for early in 1969 was concocted when the visit to South Africa was abandoned – and it turned out to be a fiasco. Pakistan was in political turmoil and cricket became a pawn in the country's own private game. Rioting broke out on the first day of the first Test, which was drawn. Colin made a century against a backdrop of student unrest; he was jostled on the field by spectators. The second Test, also drawn, was likewise interrupted. The third Test was abandoned before the first innings was completed, by when Colin was bemused by the absurdity of it all. 'He found the making of decisions more and more bewildering in the circumstances,' reported *Wisden*. He had, in fact, wanted to take his team home earlier than they went, believing them to be in physical danger, but Ames, again his manager, had insisted they stick by the advice of the Foreign Office, which was that they should remain in the country. The Foreign Office feared recrimination against the English population if they pulled out. Colin was informed, too, during the third Test that Stuart Chiesman had died. He then flew home immediately, at the end of the second day's play. All told, it was a sad finale to what proved to be the last occasion on which he captained England.

The climax to Colin's career, or so he envisaged it, would be to lead England against South Africa in 1970 and then regain the Ashes from Australia in 1970–1. It would be a fair, if hypothetical, assumption that had he remained fit and South Africa's tour not been cancelled, he would have retained the captaincy and attained those twin objectives. He had lost nothing as a batsman or in enthusiasm.

Alas, his achilles tendon injury shattered his plan. He was left, in the summer of 1969, not with the captaincy of England against New Zealand and West Indies, but to recuperate and start his memoirs. Although he was quite capable of writing these himself and had already written three books plus various articles for magazines such as *The Cricketer* and *Country Life*, he enlisted the help of the *Daily Mail*'s renowned sports features writer, Ian Wooldridge, and a cricketer-cum-journalist in Tony Lewis. As he attempted to sort out, as he put it, 'the wood from the trees', he could have reasonably expected then to return as England captain the following season: there had, after all, been the precedent that he, Colin, had been the caretaker for May, whose primacy he had accepted.

Thus Colin determined to become as fit as he could hope to be at an advanced age for a sportsman. There being no M.C.C. tour in the winter of 1969, he went on two minor trips with the Cavaliers and the Duke of Norfolk's XI, both to West Indies, and batted well. For a while he gave up golf with Brian Huggett, the Ryder Cup player and his neighbour, in spite of his handicap of five. He reasoned that racquets with Christopher, who was due to compete in the Public Schools championship, would make him fitter. He also played some squash. All he needed now was a run of form. When the 1970 season began, he was out of touch to the extent that he was not chosen for the first unofficial Test against a strong Rest of the World XI, which was replacing South Africa. Had he been in reasonable form or had there been no Test cricket that summer after South Africa's tour had been called off, Colin would probably have taken M.C.C. to Australia. Not only had he beaten West Indies in the Caribbean, but his claims as a player were far superior to those of Illingworth, who had had moderate success abroad. Hypotheses, though, were of little value to Colin when Illingworth was in possession of the captaincy and was chosen to lead England for the second match against Rest of the World, with Colin a player under him. The issue became, inevitably, a daily talking point.

Colin loathed this form of sparring, especially when it surfaced in the press. He had had a bellyful of it when comparisons were made between him and Close. The press were soon focusing on the disparities between himself and Illingworth. They were almost spectacularly different in background, lifestyle and attitude. The contrasts drawn up between north and south and professional and amateur were stark, if not quite to the extent that they were in the 1950s, before the advent of overseas players and the limited overs game.

Colin's relationship with Illingworth was not an easy one, just as it was not with Close. They had clashed on the 1962–63 M.C.C. tour of Australia when Illingworth, bluntly spoken where Colin was reticent, argued with him over his attendance at nets and then again over twelfth-man duties, when Illingworth had had a week in a sick bed and felt unable to field. Colin, having told him no-one else was available, had taken Penny to the premiere of a film. He was not enamoured, either, with the difference in lifestyle between amateurs and professionals. 'There was the feeling,' said Illingworth, 'that the amateur could do what he wanted. People did not like them getting more out of the game than the pros and Colin was not trusted. What he lacked as a batsman came through in his captaincy. He was not able to tell a person straight to his face what he was thinking.'

During the third Test against Rest of the World, Illingworth was appointed captain for Australia: his performances as both player, where he surpassed all expectations with the bat, and captain ultimately gave the selectors little option. He was given no choice as to his vice-captain – he was told it was to be Colin. For his part, Colin was uncertain. Unable to fulfil his greatest remaining ambition, he was disappointed to the extent of making a public apology to a Kent crowd for 'having let you down'. Not only was he unsure whether he should accept the vice-captaincy for a fourth time, he did not know whether Illingworth would accept him. Was it not offered merely to placate him, and was it not time for a younger man to be given this task? His natural and understandable disappointment was compounded by Illingworth being his successor. Anyone else and he would not have been quite so hurt.

Illingworth wrote to Colin on the recommendation of the selectors, saying that he appreciated they had had their differences in the past but that they ought to put them behind them for the good of the game. He, though, was not keen on Colin becoming vice-captain – he would have preferred Geoff Boycott – just as he was aware that Colin had his reservations. Their differences, too, were not helped by Penny, who was reported as declaring through the medium of the press that Colin would have been made captain had he been born in a semi-detached in Bradford. Illingworth, not surprisingly, resented this, and felt, since Colin had taken several days to make up his mind, that he should not have accepted the vice-captaincy at all.

Years later Alec Bedser, the then chairman of selectors, wrote of this in *Twin Ambitions*: 'One of our fears was that Colin, as a Test captain, had given the impression of lacking confidence and firmness at arriving at an important decision. As the days passed without any response from him [re the vice-captaincy] he seemed to be supplying proof of that very misgiving.' Denied realising his ambition, Colin underwent the unhappiest tour of his career. He and Illingworth exchanged minimal conversation. The opening line of one feature article at the time, accompanied by a photograph of him missing a straightforward catch, read: 'Disappointment and disillusionment have stalked Colin Cowdrey all his life . . . .'

David Clark, Colin's first captain of Kent, made up, as tour manager, a trinity which was never likely to be of kindred spirits. He had been appointed originally, it seemed, with a view to Colin becoming captain. From the outset this combination did not gel and as unhappy incidents proliferated, they grew further estranged. Off the field Colin largely went his own way; on it he completely lost his form, both with the bat and in the field. He spent hours shuffling around the crease and put down catches he would normally have pocketed with alacrity. Had it not been for his massed ranks of friends all around the country, he would have cut a lonely figure indeed. Some of the senior players clearly preferred Illingworth's more aggressive style of captaincy, leading Colin to say on one occasion to Clark: 'I'm just not wanted.' They were more truculent under Illingworth than they would have been under Colin's temperate leadership. Colin lost his place in the side and perked up only when the New Zealand leg of the tour began. The running of net practice in Australia, often the responsibility of the vice-captain, was handed over to Boycott and Edrich. 'There were days when Colin did not turn up to the nets at all,' said Illingworth. 'I expected him to be organising them. David Clark, a Kent man himself, did not know where he was either.'

There were players in the party who sympathised with Colin, along with sections of the press and the manager, who had been appointed at a time when it appeared conceivable that Colin would lead the party. Clark and Colin would doubtless have made an effective pairing. As it was, Clark and Illingworth had numerous differences, culminating in a dispute over the addition of an extra Test to compensate for the third Test having been washed out over Christmas. Colin was aligned on this matter, as on others, with Clark.

'I believe it was entirely due to Cowdrey's unhappiness at being overlooked for the captaincy that his form disintegrated,' said Keith Fletcher. 'At his age and at his high level of ability, he needed a personal motivation to do well in a Test series, and playing under Illingworth seemed a deterrent rather than a spur. He appeared to be thoroughly morose towards the end of the trip. Their antipathy created two camps, a most unhealthy situation for any tour team. If I was closer to Illingworth, it was because I preferred the way in which he played the game. Cowdrey, to my mind, inspired his own side in no other way than his personal contribution with the bat. Illingworth knew, quite simply, how to go about winning at Test cricket.'

Having regained the Ashes, Illingworth naturally retained the captaincy – and did not lose it until 1973. By then not even Colin, who relinquished the leadership of Kent in 1971, could have anticipated captaining his country again. Of the 27 occasions on which he led England over a decade, he was victorious in eight Tests and defeated four times. There is a saying that it is not how you lead that matters, but when and against whom. He was pitted against strong West Indies sides in ten of those matches and against varied Australian opposition in a further six matches. As a counter-balance, the Indians of 1959, the South Africans of 1960 and the Pakistanis of 1962 were weak. It is a fair record, especially by comparison with more recent England captains, but it did not, on the whole, temper the estimations of players who competed with and against Colin, nor of those who sat in the selectorial sanctum.

Chapter Six

Turbulence and Triumph

S O COLIN'S FIVE-YEAR plan for success as England captain, which had begun so promisingly in West Indies in 1967–68, had finally been scuppered by events chiefly beyond his control: rain, injury and politics. He could, it was true, have pushed for the original inclusion of Basil D'Oliveira in his M.C.C. party for South Africa in 1968–69, but it remains speculative whether that would have made one iota of difference to subsequent events. It was as a result of South Africa's Premier, John Vorster, objecting to the eventual, late inclusion of D'Oliveira that the tour was cancelled. Only one cricketer knew more than him about the ramifications of what became known as the D'Oliveira affair. That cricketer was Colin Cowdrey.

In politics as in character, Colin is essentially conservative. Harold Wilson's Labour Government was in power in 1968, and the Sports Minister, Denis Howell, had told the House of Commons the previous year that the tour to South Africa would be called off if there were any attempts to ban D'Oliveira, a Cape Coloured. Colin, though, sought guidance as to his selection from the shadow Foreign Secretary, who was also a former President of M.C.C. He was friendly with Sir Alec Douglas-Home, as he was with Ted Heath, then the leader of the Opposition. Douglas-Home had spoken to Dr Vorster, and during the first Test of the 1968 summer told Colin that as (presumed) captain he must choose the strongest M.C.C. party which was available, whether or not it included D'Oliveira. 'He told me that my course of action was absolutely clear,' wrote Colin in *M.C.C.*. 'I must be absolutely honest and straightforward about it and not deviate. Sir Alec could not say whether D'Oliveira would be accepted or not. No-one in the world could say what the political climate would be in October.' M.C.C. accepted his viewpoint. Colin introduced

*A different kind of follow through. Colin playing golf in the Croydon and District Alliance 27-holes four-ball event. (*The Times *photo library)*

D'Oliveira to Douglas-Home during the course of that match, in which D'Oliveira batted exceptionally well. 'He told me to concentrate on cricket and not to become involved in politics,' said D'Oliveira.

Colin said later that he accepted the captaincy for South Africa only after being given assurances that the party would be chosen on cricketing ability alone. He said it had been made clear to him that if a coloured cricketer was chosen and the South African Government objected, the tour would be called off immediately and the responsibility would rest entirely with South Africa. 'Sport is still one of the most effective bridges in linking people,' he explained, 'and I am convinced it is right that I should lead M.C.C. to South Africa.' He had his critics, those who argued that since he had made no secret of his dislike of apartheid, he should have nothing to do with a tour of South Africa.

At the time, D'Oliveira did not know Colin well. He had seen him play once on his sole tour of South Africa in 1956–57 and had met him only two years prior to 1968, when they both played against West Indies. They had not exchanged a word in opposition at county level before that. They got on well in spite of Colin's initial reservations about D'Oliveira's game, which was so very different from his own. Based on a short backlift, a good eye and muscular forearms, it had been learned on the bouncy matting strips that the Cape Coloureds used in the Republic. Under Colin's captaincy, D'Oliveira had not had much success in the Caribbean in 1967–68: if he were to return to his native land as an English Test cricketer, which was his fervent ambition, he had to make an impact against Australia.

D'Oliveira, for his part, liked Colin and respected his captaincy and batting. Colin and Peter May had been the two England cricketers D'Oliveira had wanted to see when he sat at deep fine-leg in the segregated section of Newlands in Cape Town, a ground where he himself was never permitted to play owing to the colour of his skin. He found Colin to be a highly intelligent, thoughtful man who was prepared to listen. When Colin left him out of the second Test against Australia in 1968, D'Oliveira trusted him that it was for cricketing reasons and not, as cynical voices were quick to suggest, for expedient political motives. He had made an undefeated 87 in the first Test but was dropped so that England could include Barry Knight as the third seamer. There were forebodings in the guise of a prediction from Lord Cobham, a former president of M.C.C., that the tour would probably have to be cancelled if D'Oliveira were included, and a businessman offered him a contract to coach in South Africa – provided he announced he would be unavailable for the tour. The third and fourth Tests passed by without D'Oliveira being included. 'I trusted Colin as a gentleman and his words kept coming back to me that I would be back soon, but deep down I was conscious that there was now something bigger at stake than just the wishes of an ordinary professional cricketer. However much I trusted that I would get a square deal in England, I knew other factors occasionally determined that certain individuals became irrelevant and unimportant,' said D'Oliveira. The evening before he had been left out of the side for the Second Test D'Oliveira had been told by a leading cricket official that the only way the tour could be saved was if he announced he was unavailable to play for England but would like to be chosen for South Africa instead.

It was, in fact, Colin himself who inadvertently started the D'Oliveira affair. In the week before the fifth Test was to begin at the Oval, he played there for Kent, taking a hundred off Surrey. It was not the fast bowlers but the medium-pacers, notably Alan Dixon, who disconcerted the batsmen. With this in mind, Colin asked his fellow England selectors, on choosing the side for the fifth Test, whether he could go for a medium-pacer in addition to the pace attack they had settled upon. The selectors agreed. Tom Cartwright would be first choice, Barry Knight second choice and D'Oliveira in reserve.

As fate would have it, the first two did not recover from injury in time to play. D'Oliveira was drafted into England's twelve the day before the Test started, with no explanation from Colin or any other selector as to why this was the case. When, by another extraordinary turn of events Roger Prideaux dropped out of the side with pleurisy, D'Oliveira became certain to play, primarily now for his batting. The rest is history. As convinced as he was determined that he would make a century, he scored 158. Colin described it as 'a remarkable innings, he really is a most remarkable person'. The stroke with which D'Oliveira reached his century was, he admitted, pinched from Colin – the paddle to leg against the slow bowler, in this instance John Gleeson. He then made a vital breakthrough on the final day, helping England to win the match.

D'Oliveira said, and wrote in his autobiography, *Time to Declare*, that a conversation with Colin had confirmed his optimism that he would be chosen for the tour party. 'He told me how well I'd done, that he was delighted I'd made a successful comeback and that in his opinion I ought to go on the tour. As captain of the side, he wanted to know what would be my feelings about playing at Newlands, at the Wanderers' stadium in Johannesburg, how would the media behave towards me. I think I reassured him; I said I wouldn't be making any press statements, that I would leave all that to the manager and captain and that I would be extremely careful about where I went throughout the tour. Colin said he would accept full responsibility for me and he would tell the England selectors so.' He satisfied Colin that his presence would not be an embarrassment to M.C.C. or to the South Africans. They tried to envisage all possible difficulties and parted with D'Oliveira under the impression that, in the event of the issue of racial discrimination being raised at the selection meeting, Colin would not remain in the room.

In *M.C.C.*, Colin wrote: 'D'Oliveira himself, I am sure, believed he had done enough to justify his selection for the tour. On purely cricketing grounds I was not so sure.' Neither, it seemed, were the other selectors. The tour party was duly announced after the fifth Test – and D'Oliveira's name was absent, omitted by a six-man team of selectors with M.C.C. officers in attendance. Colin's was but one voice (and privately he had been assured by the other selectors that, if a replacement was required, he would be able to call upon D'Oliveira) yet press and public came down upon Colin in a way that he had not experienced since the row over his national service. There were calls that he should stand down as captain. Penny sent D'Oliveira's wife flowers with the message 'Thinking of you very much today. Love to you both' – and it was a gesture which in itself made national news. Colin himself did not contact the banished all-rounder: he had no wish to inflame the situation further in the eyes of the media. His statement that the racial issue was never discussed at the selection meeting had not found a chord.

Yet this was all redeemable. When Cartwright dropped out of the tour party with recurring injury problems, D'Oliveira was the replacement. Amidst the kerfuffle that this caused, and before there was a reaction from Pretoria, an allegation was made in London that D'Oliveira had accepted a payment from SANROC – South Africa Non-Racial Open Committee for Olympic Sports – with whom he had had his differences as to how to bring about the ending of apartheid. On hearing this, he approached Colin, believing that he should be kept informed. 'It would have been too embarrassing for him to have been confronted with the rumour, perhaps in a public place, or even issuing from some high authority,' said D'Oliveira. 'He had always shown extreme courtesy towards me and his faith had been severely tested by forces which sought to toss me aside. I imagine that he supported me because he believed in my cricket and knew I was not using it for mischievous purposes.' D'Oliveira knew that if Colin thought he wanted to use his position in the public eye for political ends, Colin would have vanquished him. D'Oliveira had no doubts that Colin would believe his denial of this rumour. 'But I felt he was entitled to know how vulnerable I was to a smear campaign.'

The following day Dr Vorster, speaking from the Afrikaaner stronghold of Bloemfontein, cancelled the tour. D'Oliveira, dignified throughout and certain in his own mind that Colin had wanted him originally, drove down to see him. 'Not at any time did he even hint at the matters which had been discussed at the meetings he had attended, but he was a shoulder to lean on during the whole business and he still hoped he could save the tour by flying out to South Africa to talk to Dr Vorster,' said D'Oliveira. 'He was very upset that it was called off. When we ended up at Kandy that winter instead of South Africa he sat next to me in a cattle truck and said how sorry he was for me. He knew the incident would never leave me.' Colin and Billy Griffith, M.C.C.'s secretary, had even been asked from South Africa whether there was any chance of D'Oliveira withdrawing through a 'diplomatic illness', which would enable the tour to go ahead. Both denounced the suggestion.

In writing a foreword to *The D'Oliveira Affair*, Colin mentioned that he had asked D'Oliveira whether he could go through it all again. 'Significantly, he replied that, although he would not dream of choosing any other walk of life and was relieved to have come through the turmoil, never . . . never . . . never again! Rather sad, tragic in fact, that such a magnificent games player, so good-natured, will always sense this shadow over his moments of greatest triumph.' To this day, Colin treasures D'Oliveira's fair-mindedness and diplomacy in not criticising M.C.C., as so many did; or, for that matter, any other individual or body.

At the time, Ted Dexter wrote: 'We will never know the whole truth concerning the omission of D'Oliveira from the M.C.C. touring party to South Africa . . . . I come down on the side of honesty, a good honest piece of bungling by good honest men.' No vote was recorded at the selection meeting and, even if it were, it would not tell of whether, consciously or sub-consciously, the selectors were affected by knowing that D'Oliveira's inclusion would put the tour in jeopardy.

Colin's original draft of the issue for inclusion in *M.C.C.* never appeared in print. He sent a copy to Douglas-Home for his perusal. On summoning Colin and Wooldridge to see him, Douglas-Home queried some of his comments. 'Did I really say that?' he asked. The relevant chapter was subsequently re-written.

In 1970, Colin believed, staunchly, that South Africa's tour of England should go ahead. In an interview with the *Daily Mail*, he said: 'I say to myself, what good can come from a cancellation? I'm not an intellectual, nor do I read extensively, but I cannot reconcile an isolation policy and boycott with the Christian ethic. I agree that the effect on the Commonwealth Games might be disastrous, and that would be very sad indeed for me. But that responsible and supposedly civilised people should threaten this type of blackmail when they say they will not compete in the Games if we play South Africa is petty, spineless and pathetic. Put it the other way. I can't think of any cricketer who would be so proud of such blackmail by saying they wouldn't play against a team from another country because South Africa was taking part in the Commonwealth Games.

'I think the South African players who have been playing over here with the Cavaliers and have seen integrated living as it should be are desperately thoughtful about their system back home. I hope that they go back to South Africa, as did the Springbok rugby players, very much affected by our deep feelings in this country against their system of apartheid.'

Shortly after that interview, the tour was cancelled. The following year Colin had a further stab at resuming cricketing relations. He spent several weeks in the autumn and winter of 1971 trying to make arrangements to take a strong multi-racial side to South Africa in February and March of 1972. The idea that they should play against both white and non-white teams was mooted with Jack Cheetham, president of the South African Cricket Association, who three years earlier had flown to London specially to apologise to M.C.C. for Dr Vorster's cancellation of the 1968–69 tour.

Colin's plans had the backing, as opposed to the blessing, of the Cricket Council, which incorporated M.C.C. and the Test and County Cricket Board. He flew to the Republic to have exploratory talks with Hassan Howa, president of the South African Cricket Board, which represented non-white cricketers. His intention was to include both D'Oliveira and Ron Headley, a West Indian who played for Worcestershire. Without D'Oliveira, Colin's party would be palpably incomplete. 'With him and playing against non-white sides, bridges could be crossed that have long been impassable,' wrote John Woodcock in *The Times*. Large crowds would be attracted and it would maintain interest in cricket which was bound to be affected by the cancellation of another tour, that by South Africa to Australia. D'Oliveira was keen to go, 'if there was a joint invitation from all the cricket associations of South Africa including the coloured groups and I knew in advance the conditions under which I would be going and who and where we would be playing.' The South African Government had intimated they would be agreeable to Colin's side in their country.

The stumbling block was the reluctance of the S.A.C.B. to compromise their attitudes. They believed that to raise an

Colin in the pulpit at St James, Piccadilly. He would also preach during M.C.C. tours. (Keystone Press Agency)

all-coloured side to play a visiting team, even if the visitors were multi-racial, was an extension of racialism. They did not see it as a progressive step. Howa said that he was in favour of all cricket in South Africa coming under the authority of one multi-racial ruling body 'only if from the start non-whites have equal representation'. The S.A.C.B. exerted pressure on D'Oliveira to withdraw and thereafter interest in the tour fell away. Colin did not wish to go ahead without Howa's blessing and, even though black cricketers would still have been prepared to tour, he called it off.

There the matter rested, although Colin remained optimistic that cricket between England and South Africa would be resumed in his lifetime. He knew that D'Oliveira's standpoint

– 'sport is no longer the issue' – was the reality. The two remain in contact, although they have not touched on South Africa since the 1970s. This, in spite of Colin's standing and influence within the International Cricket Council.

Other than captaining M.C.C. in Australia and scoring one hundred hundreds, there was only one remaining goal for Colin at the beginning of 1970. Kent had not won the county championship for 57 years and, it seemed, they would never have a better opportunity to do so again. A young side had matured rapidly. In 1967 and 1968 they finished runners-up to Yorkshire but in 1969 slipped from second place to tenth, their lowest position since 1963. Colin, of course, had missed much of 1969 through injury. The following year the county committee, sadly shorn of Chiesman, decided to gamble. They increased the staff, already a strong one with seven Test players on it, in the hope of achieving greater success and hence increased attendances.

The omens for the season were auspicious. It was Kent's centenary year. The President was Lord Harris, whose father had exercised dominion over Kent cricket to an extent which even Colin could not equal. Then at the centenary dinner Ted Heath made the most prophetic of speeches. As a boy he had cycled from his home town of Broadstairs to the St Lawrence ground at Canterbury. His father, a master builder, had known Stuart Chiesman through carrying out work for him at Chiesman's house in nearby Kingsgate. As Leader of the Opposition, Heath still managed to maintain a close interest in cricket. At the dinner he said that he thought 1906 had been Kent's most significant year to date: there had been a change of Government and Kent had won the championship for the first time. Now, come 1970, surely there was going to be a repeat?

Colin was fully fit again after his achilles tendon injury the previous year. Yet he began the season disastrously, and so did Kent. They lost two of their first three championship matches to Glamorgan and to Warwickshire, beaten by the latter through Rohan Kanhai's brilliant century. Colin made just 152 runs in his first thirteen innings. On a deteriorating pitch at Dover, on which Kent were beaten by an innings by Northamptonshire, Colin bagged a pair in one day; subsequently Alec Bedser, the chairman of selectors, telephoned him to say he would not be included for England's first 'Test' against Rest of the World. Of their next five matches, Kent won just one. They had garnered a paltry thirteen batting points and languished near the foot of the table. And this before the inevitable Test calls came.

Colin finally found his form during Tunbridge Wells week in June, making hundreds in both matches against Sussex and Essex, but neither was won and by July, when Kent were beaten badly in the first round of the Gillette Cup by Sussex, they were bottom of the table. Surrey, the leaders, had more than double their 58 points. The crowds were falling away and it looked as if the club was in for a considerable financial loss. At that point Ames, the secretary-manager, called a team meeting in the dressing-room at Mote Park, Maidstone, at which everyone was invited to speak his mind. 'He produced an old-fashioned broadside,' said Colin. It had the desired effect. Secretary-manager and players resolved in particular to go flat out for bonus batting points.

The county's strength lay primarily in its attacking batsmen. Mike Denness and Brian Luckhurst complemented each other as opening batsmen. Denness, a future England captain, had had a trying period with Colin when he came south to join them from his home in Ayrshire. In a speech at a dinner in Dartford at the end of his first season, 1962, he had said that Kent had one of the best batsmen in the country in Colin and were looking to him to win matches. The speech made the press, was interpreted as criticism of Colin, and consequently reports reached Colin in Australia and Chiesman, whose reaction was along the lines of 'this fly-by-night who's come across Hadrian's Wall'. Denness had to wait until Colin returned in the spring to sort out the misunderstanding. It was resolved; Colin became godfather to Denness's elder daughter; Denness became vice-captain to Colin. He was by 1970 an England cricketer, as was Luckhurst, who, although more aligned to Illingworth's style of captaincy, appreciated Colin's advice and toleration when things went wrong. As a pair they made for the best opening partnership in the country. Then there was Asif Iqbal, a free-scoring batsman of world class who came

107

to Kent after being much impressed by the attitude of Colin, Knott and Underwood when playing for Pakistan during 1967. 'Colin appreciated my cricket from first slip and would say to me between overs, "How do you play such shots?" There was no swearing. I was approached to play for Kent by Colin and although the offer was not the best I received, I accepted because of what I had seen of those three.' When Asif joined Kent in 1968, Colin would think nothing of collecting him from his Orpington home and ferrying him to matches, enjoying the irony of having a Pakistani map-reading for him in England. It left a lasting impression: 'I used to tell my kids that Colin had achieved so much yet he always had time for others – that was what made him so respected,' said Asif.

Without Asif, Kent would not have been anything like so successful. There was an air of expectancy every time he walked to the crease. He, Graham Johnson, John Shepherd and Bob Woolmer could bat almost anywhere in the order and make their runs quickly; and as young players Colin ensured they were looked after. He and Ames had spotted Shepherd in Barbados – Keith Boyce, who joined Essex, was their first choice – and he had become one of the most consistent all-rounders in English cricket. Colin was to find winter employment for Johnson, whom he introduced to one of his banking contacts at the National Bank of South Africa, which he hoped would keep him in the game. Woolmer, if anything, overdid moulding himself on Colin, who was his boyhood hero. Yet he was clearly a player of potential and was capped during the season, as was Johnson.

Alan Ealham, another who was capped, was the best out-fielder Colin ever saw, high praise indeed; and a stocky hard-hitting middle-order batsman. He and Stuart Leary, a South African who had played football for Charlton and whose rapid wit was sometimes too much for Colin, could thrash the ball about them in the middle of an innings. Then there was Alan Knott, the best wicket-keeper in the world and an unselfish improviser who was prepared to accept going in low in the order, sometimes lower than he did for England. They could, and should, bat without inhibition. From Maidstone week onwards Kent began to gain a plentiful supply of bonus points.

Six were obtained from the first match of the week, a draw against Derbyshire in which Colin scored a masterly 76. Then against Hampshire, when Colin had returned to Test match duty, Kent achieved a victory through their seamers who, with the exception of Shepherd, compensated through containment what they may have lacked in penetration. Graham, Dye and Brown were supported by Woolmer, who, before his back trouble was able to swing the ball markedly. For spin there was Underwood, not yet at the peak of his career but of inestimable value. That season he took 78 wickets, enough for everybody but himself. Johnson was developing into a tidy off-spinner. As an all-rounder he replaced Alan Dixon, whose last season it was. Dixon had been an effective vice-captain, not afraid to speak his mind to Colin. He also had a cutting sense of humour. 'Twinkle, twinkle little star', he sang once when Colin came into the dressing-room undefeated after an innings which had not impressed him. He still finished up as coach at Tonbridge.

When Colin was absent, the reserves performed highly creditably under Denness. Against Essex at Harlow he made an unbeaten century in a match Kent won by an innings. His example was total in going for quick runs. Next, Yorkshire had the better of a drawn match before Colin, returning to Kent after being passed over for the captaincy of M.C.C. to Australia, played the ideal innings in difficult conditions against Sussex at Hove. He made 77, put on 154 with Luckhurst and Kent won the match by ten wickets. Both matches in Canterbury week were drawn but notable victories ensued against Somerset and Gloucestershire. On a poor pitch at Cheltenham Kent made 340 to win after avoiding the follow-on by one run. Asif made 109, Denness 97.

Kent were now immersed in the championship race, yet Colin's caution prevailed. He suggested to Asif that it was a pity the season could not be extended, since they might then triumph. Asif, astonished, said: 'I've already told Mike Denness we shall win it in our last match at the Oval.' Colin thought it was a flight of fantasy. However, after a rain-affected draw against Northamptonshire, Kent won their following three matches. Surrey, fellow championship contenders, were beaten by twelve runs in the penultimate over of a match in

Colin pulling. Not quite the classical Cowdrey, but it was a one-day match. (Patrick Eagar)

which Johnson took 12 wickets. The climax was when Pat Pocock attempted to lift him for six and was breathtakingly caught by Asif on the long-on boundary. Colin was unbeaten in both innings, making 49 and 56.

Kent then won both their matches at Folkestone, the first against a Nottinghamshire side which included Sobers. Just as at Dover two years before, he made the most superb century and, as it was also his nature to do, his declaration on the last day ensured the opposition would have a chance. It was a stiffer target than he had left Colin in Trinidad; but on a true pitch Kent reached it. They needed 282 in three hours and won with eight balls to spare, Knott striking three fours at the death. Their second match of the week pitted them against Leicestershire and Ray Illingworth on another excellent pitch. Now, the quest for bonus points reached a crescendo. Having taken five by bowling out Leicestershire for 152, Kent then obtained eight for batting through making 421 for seven and gaining the eighth point off the 85th over of the innings, the last from which it could be taken. Johnson and Shepherd smote 21 runs off that over. Underwood then bowled Kent to victory before lunch on the final day. Kent took 23 points in all and for them and Colin, it was a second victory over Illingworth that season.

Those two results meant Kent would most likely only have to take bonus points from their last match, against Surrey at the Oval, to ensure them of the championship pennant. They gained four for bowling and four for batting the following day through Colin himself making a century. It was, he said later, one of the best he had scored in England, made on a grassy pitch which was giving the bowlers significant help. Lancashire would need to take 27 points from their last match, also against Surrey, to overtake Kent, and Colin for one believed it could not be done. There is a familiar photograph of him on the Oval balcony, a beaming smile on those rotund features, dispensing hops to Kent supporters gathered below. His optimism was shared by Heath, now the Prime Minister, who was in the dressing-room sharing the champagne. He was to proffer invitations to the players to the Carlton Club and 10 Downing Street — at which Colin made, by all accounts, an impressive speech.

On the same day Heath was toasting him with champagne, Colin was asked as to his future plans by the press. His response was, surprisingly for him, spontaneous. He replied that he would retire from the captaincy of Kent at the end of the 1971 season. It meant that he would equal the record of Lord Harris, who led Kent for fifteen years – and it also signalled that his career was winding down. It is unlikely that his plans would have been altered if he had been asked to take M.C.C. to Australia since, in all probability, he would have retired from Test cricket at the end of the tour. There seemed little point in him remaining as captain of Kent for a further season: He had reached his goal and, unless Kent won the championship again, 1971 would be anti-climactic. This was what occurred, partly on account of his missing much of the season through serious pneumonia.

Had he continued as captain until his retirement he would not have experienced the difficulties which arose through a difference of opinion with his successor as to how often and in what competitions he should play. Yet it was a good time, and an unselfish time, to hand over, for Kent were clearly going to win further competitions. Colin may have made his decision lightly, but he was not going back on it.

Chapter Seven

Swansong Postponed

I**N HIS LAST YEARS** in County cricket, Colin batted about as
well as he had ever done. He may have shuffled at the crease
and struggled in the field if he was moved out of the slips in
limited-overs cricket, but his technique remained unimpaired.
His form for Kent in 1971 was such that England could not leave
him out at the start of the season. He was excelling in both the
County championship – he made 605 runs in 14 innings before
he went down with pneumonia – and the one-day game. He did
not play at all in the second half of the season but planned,
nevertheless, to continue playing for two more years. Ames paid
tribute to him by stating that 'through his enthusiasm, example
and dedication, the fortunes of the county had improved'. Colin
was relinquishing the captaincy of a side the equal of any in the
country.

Before the start of the 1972 season, Colin was awarded the
C.B.E. Penny, Christopher and Jeremy accompanied him to
Buckingham Palace to receive it. This enhanced his enthusiasm for the summer ahead. Indeed, he was as keen as mustard.
He played mainly in the championship matches, reaching
1,000 runs without being called up to play Test cricket. He
found himself often left out of one-day cricket by Denness,
who reasoned that to have him and Luckhurst at the crease
together could result in the innings becoming becalmed. In
1973 there were occasions when he was left out of the side
altogether. Denness felt at times that he had to choose between
Colin and a younger player in need of experience: it was not a
situation which he, Denness, would have liked to have been in.
The temptation to omit Colin was an obvious one: Colin had
turned 40 and a younger batsman, in addition to being more
mobile in the field, might well score his runs more quickly in
the middle of the order. He would most probably not score as
many or make them as classically as Colin, but he would be
prepared to throw caution to the winds and that, when there

were bonus points at issue, was what counted. Ealham, who would never be anything like as good a batsman as Colin, often went in above him at this time. Peter May touched on this in his foreword to *M.C.C.*: 'I am afraid I could never understand how any selectors could consider leaving Colin out of the side whatever duration of the game was involved – as for ever asking him to bat down the order after batsmen who weren't worthy of buckling his pads – I just could not comprehend it.'

By Maidstone week in the middle of the summer, Colin was batting at number six. Against Somerset he made the 99th century of his career in four and three-quarter hours. In the second match of the week, against Surrey, he went in at number seven just before lunch on the second day. He had often joked to Asif Iqbal, with whom he was batting in the afternoon, that one day he would be as quick as him between the wickets: Asif was about as nimble a runner as it was possible to be. They batted together until tea, when Colin was a handful of runs away from his 100th hundred. Then twice in the nineties he was beaten outside off-stump. 'I tried to relax him by going down the pitch and telling him that he had appeared to play at the ball,' said Asif. 'But I could see the tension in his eyes. When he reached 99 I told him to push the ball anywhere and I would run.' Colin did not think there was any hope of a single when he prodded the ball into the covers, but before he could call Asif had set off.

Scrambling to the other end, Colin hid his face, as if to ask Asif how he had managed to scamper 22 yards. The declaration followed immediately, the crowd giving Colin a tumultuous reception as he returned to champagne in the pavilion. He gave Asif two tankards with inscribed details of their partnership and sent wine to the press box, even to the correspondent who reported that he had pushed his 100th run to the leg-side. He was the third Kent cricketer to have achieved this feat – he, Frank Woolley and Les Ames made 354 first-class hundreds between them. It should, Ames felt, have been more. Appreciative though he was of Colin's achievement, it was to his surprise that Colin did not make 200 hundreds in all.

After that, Colin normally went in at number five in 1973. Although he had not played in any of Kent's preceding Benson and Hedges matches, his form was such that he could hardly be left out of the final later that month against Worcestershire. Reverting to number seven, he made 29 out of 53 off the last eight overs through some deft placement. It helped Kent to win the match. Yet in 1974 he began the season batting down the order again, albeit in a side in which the two West Indian all-rounders, Bernard Julien and John Shepherd, were going in at numbers nine and ten. Against Hampshire at Basingstoke Colin was hit on the head as he shaped to hook Andy Roberts, another West Indian bowler, on a dodgy pitch: he fell on his stumps and took no further part in the match. He recuperated with a fine century in more trusted conditions at Fenner's and subsequently retained his position at number three. He finished the season with 1,000 runs and was playing well enough, he felt, to be included in M.C.C.'s party to tour Australia and New Zealand under Denness.

Indeed, even though he was almost 42 and had not played for England since 1971, he was saddened not to be included. Yet he had to wait only until December. So battered by Australia's fast bowlers were M.C.C. that they turned to Colin when it reached the stage that, because of injuries, they would have to recruit another batsman from England. The management pair of Alec Bedser, chairman of selectors, and Alan Smith, plus the senior players, Denness, John Edrich and Tony Greig, all plumped for him. They felt that not only would he be the batsman most capable of deflecting some exceptionally fast and hostile bowling from Lillee and Thomson but that, technically, there was no-one his equal.

It was the bravest of decisions by Colin. He, along with many other cricket followers in England, had seen enough on the highlights from the first Test at Brisbane to know that Lillee was fully fit again, that in Thomson the Australians had discovered a bowler of frightening pace – and that the televised highlights were not totally misleading. They depicted Australian fast bowlers seemingly claiming a wicket each ball, the crowd howling and the batsmen trying desperately to protect their very lives. For an Englishman, it was not pleasant watching. Yet Colin was chuffed to be asked to go to his beloved Australia by the players themselves and literally dropped everything to do so – notably an instructional book on coaching he was preparing. Tony Pawson was assisting

115

Facing Roberts at Basingstoke in 1974. The bowler is clearly presenting a challenge. (Patrick Eagar)

him with it one morning at Colin's home, Kentish Border in Limpsfield, when Denness telephoned. Three days later Colin was on his way to Perth, much to the mystification of those Australians who greeted the news with ribald comments and cartoons. They scarcely ever brought anyone back and could not comprehend why, if Colin was wanted now, he had not been asked to tour originally. This opinion over-rode any admiration for his courage at being prepared to take on the bouncers once again. The press talked of Dad's Army and Santa Claus; Thomson spoke of Colin 'copping it as fast as anyone'. These reactions brought out his most wry sense of humour. 'Why should I worry?' he said. 'After all, I faced Gregory and McDonald.'

It was his sixth tour of Australia, equalling the record of Johnny Briggs, the Lancashire slow-arm bowler who toured in a very different age, between 1884–85 and 1897–98. Just before the call came, the Duke of Norfolk ventured to him, with a twinkle in his eye: 'Mr Thomson looks very fast to me, even for young 42-year-olds.' Earlier that year Colin had written in *The Cricketer*, of which he had been appointed a director, 'Watching the England batsmen striving to get on terms with themselves against West Indies in Barbados, I could not help thinking what an impact Jack Hobbs' serene temperament and faultless technique would have made on the proceedings. In blunting the sharpness of the opposition's opening attack he would have brought down the pulse rate in the English dressing-room.' For Hobbs, read Cowdrey.

On 7 December, Colin was in London. On 10 December he had his first net in Perth, after a twenty-hour delay in Bombay during the flight from England. Tony Lock, who was resident in Perth, helped him acclimatise, as did Graham McKenzie, who spent a fair part of his career opposing him on behalf of Australia. The telephone never stopped ringing for Colin, the callers well-wishers every one. They included those who, like Sir Donald Bradman, believed his task should have been given to a younger and more active cricketer.

Three days later, Colin was batting at number three in the second Test. There were serious injury problems. Both Edrich and Amiss, who would normally have been chosen ahead of Colin, were missing. Neither match fit nor properly attuned

117

Departing for Australia in December 1974. Colin is assisted by his neighbour, Brian Huggett, who drove him to Heathrow Airport. (Keystone Press Agency)

118

to the fierce and arid Australian heat, Colin formulated a plan. From his cricket bag, sprang, like bread rising from an oven, foam rubber to pad his chest and wrists. He was intent on survival, to wear down the fast bowlers through protection and his peerless technique. He would attempt to play only the straight or the loose ball, even if it meant that the bowlers would dictate to him. Soon in the fray and cheered all the way to the wicket, he dropped his wrists on the short ball, taking his bat down and across his body, swaying away from the line. At Perth, on the fastest, bounciest pitch in the world there was all too little pitched up that he could attempt to drive, but his approach and courage in getting behind the line imbued his colleagues with confidence. In two hours he made 22 before Thomson bowled him as he moved too far across his stumps. In the second innings, asked to open since Luckhurst had become the latest victim of the Australian bowlers, he had made 41 and reckoned he had just about seen off Thomson when he was out leg-before. He had put on 52 with David Lloyd, who earned Colin's everlasting gratitude for volunteering to take Lillee, bowling ferociously fast with the wind, at the start of the innings. They had given England a glimmer of a chance of saving the match – but a glimmer was all it turned out to be. As throughout the series, Australia were simply too strong.

Between the second and third Tests M.C.C. had a match against South Australia which gave Colin the opportunity for practice against a more gentle attack. Opening again, even though Edrich was now fit, he made 78. For the third Test, played at Melbourne directly after Christmas, he reverted to batting first wicket down and made 35 in three and three-quarter hours. In the second innings he scored eight as the upper order collapsed. It was not batting which was going to wrest the initiative nor change the course of the game; but in a low-scoring match against strong opposition little could. By now Colin was convinced that Lillee and Thomson were the most difficult and unpredictable pairing of fast bowlers he had ever faced. 'This confirmed,' said Denness, 'that we had encountered a new dimension in speed.' Colin's reaction to facing this was, as ever, diplomatic and enthusiastic. 'I did enjoy it so,' he said. He was less enthused with the enmity that existed between the two countries on the field. At times it was noticeable that he disapproved of some of the antics. In *Always Ready*, Ian Redpath, whom he knew quite well, wrote: 'He obviously felt things seemed to have changed since he played the bulk of his cricket and that the game was for the worse. After one incident that involved an exchange between an England and an Australian player he sidled up to me and in a tone of voice that seemed to indicate something between sadness and indignation, said, "It's just not cricket." '

In the last three Test matches of the series, Colin was unable to match his feats of endurance in the second and third Tests. He made 22 and one in the fourth Test; 26 and three in the fifth; seven in the sixth at Melbourne, his 114th and last Test. In that final innings he was batting well, he thought, on the first evening after England had dismissed Australia for 152. Amiss had gone fourth ball in poor light but Colin survived until the next morning only to be out in Walker's first over, the ball flicking his gloves on its way through to the wicket-keeper. He was bade farewell by a huge banner which read 'MCG fans thank Colin – six tours.' Colin, wearing a straw sun hat, posed beside it for photographs for young and old. He regretted, as he still does, that he was not fit enough to do himself justice and that he had not scored more runs, but he was contented with ending his career at the highest level. A few months later he was to announce his retirement.

He returned to England while the majority of the M.C.C. party went on to New Zealand. Although originally asked to go to New Zealand, he chose not to do so; he was replaced by Barry Wood, the Lancashire opener. After he returned home his battered body was nursed by a faith healer: Mrs Mary Rogers, who lived in Sussex, had been recommended to him by his old friend Cuthbert Bardsley, the Bishop of Coventry. Colin had telephoned her from Australia, asking her to pray for him and she was, he felt, responsible for curing him of various sprains.

It was axiomatic that Colin should have had some choice as to where he was to bat for Kent after he gave up the captaincy. If he was worthy of opening or going in at number three in Australia, he was equally worthy of doing so still for Kent. Yet it was not just his age which was against him

Attuning to the Australian heat and bounce. Colin in the nets at Perth shortly after arrival in 1974. (Keystone Press Agency)

121

but Kent's concentration in this period on bonus points and limited-overs cricket: pushing others up the order gave him no hope of emulating Sir Jack Hobbs and scoring a hundred hundreds in middle age. With Kent continually deprived of their leading players through Test calls, Denness reasoned that they had more chance of success in one-day rather than three-day cricket. Knott, for instance, would regularly miss ten championship matches a summer and, great trier though he was, he was seen as an England cricketer who played for Kent rather than a Kent cricketer who played for England.

This concentration on the limited-overs game – at which Denness had no little success – inevitably led to his preference for younger players. Colin could hardly be expected to take up slogging at this stage of his career and, although he had grown accustomed to batting down the order, some felt he did not belong to the modern game. Asif recalls batting with him when he stood his ground upon an appeal by Surrey players for a catch at the wicket. They roundly abused him, accusing him of cheating. 'He was not a part of that class of swearing cricketers,' said Asif.

Denness was much liked by the Kent crowds and after he retired was to become a public relations consultant; and yet during his period as captain of county and country communication was not regarded as one of his strengths. Colin felt that he was not always warned in advance that he would not be playing. Once, when Kent left the dressing-room to take the field at Trent Bridge with twelve men, Denness is alleged to have said to Colin, 'By the way, you're twelfth man.' Colin carried out his duties faithfully and adequately. Yet it was a favourite ground of his, he had been looking forward to playing and he was stung. He never quite got over it. (Denness, it should be added, has no recollection of this incident.)

Colin announced his retirement in June 1975, just months after his final Test innings. It made for national news beyond the confines of the sports pages and bulletins. He knew that, although he felt he was still good enough to play for England, he was at a disadvantage through not playing regularly for Kent. In addition, he found limited-overs cricket, when he took part in it, increasingly arduous. Tony Greig, the captain of Sussex, promptly asked him to join them to help their young players as much as their batting, and Colin mused over the idea carefully before deciding it was time to call it a day. Kent was his county and, besides, he wanted to retire at the top. He was wistful, he said, that on the horizon there was no cricket, no more tours; but he was gladdened at the prospect of a Christmas at home with his family. He did not have a productive final season – in 15 championship matches he made 591 runs – but his swansong was memorable for two matches. His unbeaten 151 against the Australians at Canterbury was, he felt, one of his greatest innings. Set 354 to win, Kent lost two early wickets and were seemingly heading for defeat before Colin and Bob Woolmer, who was intent on becoming his alter ego, turned the match. An indication of how well Colin played was that he was hooking Lillee in front of square. Kent won the match and the Australians, who had ordered dinner at their next venue, Southampton, arrived there at midnight. It was brilliant batting, and yet within a few days he had made a pair, the third of his career, against the same opposition for M.C.C. at Lord's. It was a vivid summarization of his career, of the way cricket took him to the very heights and back again.

His retirement had been announced, yet he was still given odds of twenty to one to captain England that summer. He would, no doubt, willingly have responded to the call, but this time it was not forthcoming. Greig replaced Denness as England captain and come September Colin was playing what was to have been his final innings in first-class cricket, against Surrey at the Oval. Batting at number seven and applauded all the way to the wicket, he was given one off the mark by Edrich, the captain, and Intikhab Alam, the bowler, and scored twenty in total before he was caught behind, uncharacteristically fishing outside off-stump. 'I would love to be starting out afresh,' he said, 'but with the game in its new form I could not be absolutely sure of coming over all the hurdles again.'

The Kent side which he and Ames had painstakingly built up continued to be a successful one. Yet for all the competitions that Denness won – six in five years as captain, all in limited-overs cricket – his position was tenuous. Not all the Kent players held him in high regard. He had been Chiesman's choice as vice-captain and successor to Colin. However, by the mid-1970s, with Chiesman dead and Ames having retired,

Denness was increasingly vulnerable. The new manager, Colin Page, was accountable to the secretary, Eric Attenborough, who was given heightened powers by the committee to discipline players without sanction from Denness. Colin's resentment at being omitted from 55-overs and 40-overs matches had been shared by his wife and some committee and club members. It reached the stage at which, in 1976, Denness said he would leave himself out when the committee wanted Colin to return. During one match that summer Colin, who was to be elected onto the committee, canvassed Kent's players in the dressing-room as to whether they wanted Denness to continue as captain, which led to Denness' approaching Ames with the intention of confronting Colin. But the committee had made up their minds. In the autumn, having won two trophies by the end of the summer, Denness was sacked as captain of Kent.

Colin played once for Kent in 1976, scoring 25 and fifteen against Surrey at Canterbury. He played (under Denness) and boosted the crowd, simply because the county were short of first-team players as a result of Test calls and injuries. He had hoped to play more often but was aware that this would be governed by Test calls and that there were drawbacks in a 43-year-old returning for just the odd match. This was to be his last first-class match and he was never to achieve his ambition of playing in the same Kent side as his eldest son, who joined their staff in 1976. Two years later the committee considered asking Colin to come out of retirement again and lead the side after four players including the captain, Asif, had defected to World Series Cricket, but decided such a move would only delay the development of a number of promising players – including Christopher.

Colin's illustrious contemporaries, May and Dexter, had both retired at their peak to pursue careers well remunerated. Dexter did not disguise his reasoning. 'The bills had to be paid,' he said. Chiesman's money helped Colin to live well within the simple life he liked, and to educate his children, but it was nonetheless important to him that his autobiography sold well. In the summer of 1976 *M.C.C., the Autobiography of a Cricketer* was heading the list of best-sellers. For a cricket book it was unusually long, running to 96,000 words. Apart from a chapter on Walter Robins, it was not polemical. Colin chose to send his observations on Bradman and Hutton to them for their perusal, as well as showing Douglas-Home the relevant details on D'Oliveira. Ian Wooldridge protected Colin from himself over his opinions of Illingworth. When the book was completed by Wooldridge, six years after Colin had first started work on it, Colin pronounced himself unhappy with it, much to Wooldridge's surprise. Tony Lewis, another former England captain, was enlisted to amend certain parts.

During his career, Colin had had some earning power off the field through the Bagenal Harvey organisation. Players did not promote or endorse products then to the extent that they do now, and Colin was once taken to task for advertising cigars, ostensibly because he was known to be a non-smoker of cigarettes. Underlying that, though, was the insinuation that for M.C. Cowdrey to be making money in this way was not quite cricket. He undertook some public relations work for Whitbread Fremlins, the brewers, work at which he was adept. He had no need to deploy charm: he possessed it in abundance. He joined, upon retiring, Barclays Bank International division in what effectively became a public relations role. In middle age, a time when his contemporaries from Tonbridge and Oxford were well advanced in their careers, he was having to learn new skills and a new life, as well as coping with the tedium of commuting. At least Barclays had strong links with cricket: Colin's friend Anthony Tuke, later knighted and a President of M.C.C., was its chairman and Jeffrey Stollmeyer, a former captain of West Indies, was on the board in Trinidad.

No post-war cricketer had played so much, and yet his heart still lay in the game. His enthusiasm was undiminished. To retire, even though he could, and did, continue to play at the level of wandering club player, and had time now for racquets and squash with Christopher, was a wrench. Conversely, he wondered, in his more introspective vein, whether it had all been worth while. In an unpaid article for his parish magazine, he referred to a life 'frittered away in the arena of sport'. He questioned whether an individual 'with a useful brain and fairly good reflexes and an expensive education behind him can conceivably justify having spent a quarter of a century standing at first slip. People do tend to forget that I've been at it for eleven months a year for twenty solid years and I

125

do question whether that's a justifiable way of having spent your inheritance.' He had anticipated this conflict between altruism and personal ambition almost from the outset. Early in his playing career he consulted a clergyman on the subject of whether an individual with multiple careers at his choosing could give his life to sport. The answer was an unequivocal 'yes'.

Standing at first slip rather than sitting behind a desk led to a conflict that was not of intellectual concern. In Colin's time few players opted out of tours 'for family reasons'. Only rarely did their wives join them. A legacy of twenty solid years was that Colin had seen all too little of his four children. In the summer he was playing all over England; in the winter he was away from it. 'The wives all had to ask permission to go on tours and then only those who had the means,' said Penny. 'I went three times because my father paid for me. Colin and I couldn't afford it.'

To this day Penny considers that she and not Colin taught her sons the rudiments of cricket. Kentish Border, which the Cowdreys bought in 1966, was a six-bedroomed mock-Tudor house in Limpsfield, a few miles from their previous, smaller home in Bickley. For the pentathlon that Woodcock had suggested, there was a snooker table and swimming-pool, bowling machine and ultimately a hard net in the sizeable garden. 'When the children were young it was as if we were running a country club for under-12s,' said Penny. She bowled underarm in between gardening, at which she was skilled, and laundering; Colin taught Christopher how to throw, which added to the expenditure on bread buns; Carol escaped by joining the nearest tennis club and the dog exhausted itself in pursuit of balls.

The three boys were educated at Wellesley House prep school in Broadstairs and then at Tonbridge School, following Colin there. (Chiesman would have preferred Charterhouse, where football was played.) It was at Chiesman's suggestion that they went to Wellesley; he had watched several Kent 2nd XI matches there. In the 1st XI at nine years old, Christopher was given one particular piece of cricketing advice by a master

Christopher launches into a drive, watched by Jeremy and Colin in the slips and Graham behind the wicket. (Carol Keith)

and former England squash player, Richard Boddington, which he still maintains was the best he ever received: 'When the bowler comes in, keep saying to yourself, watch the ball, watch the ball.' 'The times I've forgotten that and been out,' said Christopher. He was playing with boys three or four years his senior and excelling at all games. The school forbade newspapers and television to record his feats – the interest arose from the fact that his father was England captain for some of this period – but it welcomed Colin's occasional batting demonstrations in the nets. If he was ever severe on any one bowler, it was always a master, not a boy. He would put half a crown on his stumps and present it to the pick of the school's 1st XI bowlers. Only an exceptional batsman could, by leaving a gap between bat and pad while executing a defensive push, make a prep school boy appear to have produced an unplayable ball. Back went the off stump and the pocket money was duly handed over – as often as not to Christopher.

127

Even at Christopher's tender age, as he practised before lights out in the dormitory with a rolled up pair of socks, comparisons were made between father and son to the extent that Christopher reckoned he might fare better as a footballer. 'My father hadn't played for Chelsea and England, had he?' Promotion out of his age group inevitably meant he attracted some jealousy, leading Christopher to wonder if it really was justified by his cricketing ability. The comparisons continued when at the age of thirteen he moved to Tonbridge and, more vociferously, when he joined Kent. It was only when he played for England that he was seen, at any rate in the public's eye, as more than just the son of a famous father.

Christopher was in the Tonbridge 1st XI in his second summer at the age of fourteen: his father had been selected in his first term when thirteen. There are advantages and disadvantages about having a famous father and in Christopher's case they may well have balanced each other out. Yet the sensitivity he showed, not surprisingly, when fellow schoolboys suggested he was in the 1st XI only on account of his name, manifested itself throughout his career. There were schoolboys and Kent supporters quite prepared to say as much to his face.

When Colin went to Tonbridge, to the Head, as the 1st XI ground was known, he would often watch Christopher from behind a tree in the vain hope of not being noticed. Later he would watch Graham from the same vantage point. In Colin's presence Christopher rarely succeeded: he would be told Colin was on the ground and then almost invariably fail. Nevertheless, after a poor start, a duck against Tonbridge Town and two other low scores, he made an unbeaten 67 against Wellington and established himself in the 1st XI. In his last three years he dominated their cricket, relying more on a good eye than upon technique. Runs were easy to come by, so there was little incentive to change. In the last summer, 1975, he fell only just short of beating his father's record for the school: he made 966 runs at an average of 80 as compared with Colin's 1,033 runs at 79 in 1950. He captained sides that included Nick Kemp and Richard Ellison, both of whom joined him in playing for Kent, and in his last year, brother Jeremy.

The masters at Tonbridge believed in giving Christopher his head. Two friendships built then have lasted: with David Kemp, his god-father and housemaster at the sports-orientated Park House, and with Jonathan Smith, his tutor who collaborated on his book *Good Enough?* Kemp, who was later to serve on Kent's committee, when Christopher was captain, said: 'His popularity had little to do with his name – there was a natural modesty about him and a gregarious love of fun which went down well with everybody except the matron who had some difficulty keeping him under control.' He was not keen on doing much work and, indeed, left without gaining A-levels. 'He was neither academic nor motivated and was ingenious at finding excuses. I used to tell him he could not have a net until he had finished his work,' said Kemp. 'And then he would get down to doing it.' Nick Kemp, who was no relation, emphasised his positive nature. 'People liked him for his charisma and yet he was always Colin Cowdrey's son, never Christopher Cowdrey. I think he was overly fêted. He talked about it when we were sixteen and smoking in the bicycle sheds.' Constantly, the first comment made by parents and others to Christopher began, 'I knew your father . . . .' This would make him cringe.

It was assumed that from the age of eight Christopher would become a professional cricketer. With Graham, a strong boy and regarded as the most talented, it was from the age of six. Jeremy, two years younger than Christopher yet quicker to mature, did not have the inclination to play cricket for anything other than fun after the age of sixteen. He had been put into Tonbridge's 1st XI in his second year and had struggled because he was not as gifted as his brothers. Unlike them, he did not score a century for the school. Yet he was close to one once, at a time when John Inverarity, the former Australian cricketer, was spending a year there teaching maths and coaching cricket. At lunch, when he was in the nineties, Inverarity told him not to go to the dining-room but to stay in the pavilion and think about his innings. He was out first ball upon resumption.

It was soon apparent he would not be sucked into professional cricket. He was not of the necessary standard, so it was as well that, by the time he left Tonbridge, he had no desire to progress further in the game. He abandoned club cricket for Limpsfield when too much came to be expected of him; he took to wandering cricket on two out of three weekends in the summer, keenly but lacking in match temperament. It is the same with his golf. He likes to enjoy spare time which is precious owing to City demands, so he bowls his leg-breaks, as he did at Durham University, with generous air and an enthusiasm diminished only when expected to perform on account of being a Cowdrey.

Unlike Christopher and Graham, Jeremy has rarely found his surname to be a hindrance: he likens its benefits to the advantages a pretty girl has when entering a party. Consequently, he has had an easier life than his brothers. 'Dad feels guilty about the pressure his name has put on us,' he said. 'That's why, not being a sportsman, I am closest to him.' He was also the best judge of those who would claim friendship with the Cowdreys. Christopher was not certain who was asking him out to tea at school, the boy or the parent, and Graham found it hard to trust others; but Jeremy came to see through phoney people. 'The really nice boys shied away from me at school,' he said.

There are marked differences in character between the three but a bond has always existed between them and their sister, Carol, who had to forge her own identity while Penny chauffeured the boys to matches. Perhaps inevitably, their interests came first. Carol developed, to the bane of her school career, a reckless adolescent streak. She did not always see eye to eye with Penny. One of several schools which passed through her life was West Heath, near Sevenoaks where she was a contemporary of the Princess of Wales and rather more rebellious. It was as much to gain attention as anything else. Her father, often as not, was away from home; her mother's role was accommodating the interests of four men. As a girl on the lawn at Kentish Border she had more than her fair share of bowling and fielding. There were not many opportunities to bat. At Skinners Day at Tonbridge she would be at the Head watching the cricket, with a break only for a picnic out of the boot of the car. Her escape was the tennis court since there was a club near her home and she became a proficient player. She has a ready line for those who ask her if she has had enough of

Christopher playing in his first match at Lord's, batting for Young England against Young West Indies in 1974. (The Hulton Deutsch Collection)

131

cricket: 'I've been saturated in it.' As well as tennis, at school she played hockey, lacrosse, netball, athletics, 'anything that kept me out of the classroom. My insecurities came out there.' After leaving school, when doing a job as a tea lady in Australia, it was discovered she was a Cowdrey. She had kept quiet about her surname, in spite of Colin's popularity in the country. 'We are not the sort of family to promote ourselves because we have an old-fashioned English gentleman as our father,' she said. 'He doesn't need to say that he has made it. We developed an unwritten rule of never name-dropping: "One sniff of a name drop and you are fined."'

Where Carol was rumbustious, Graham was immured in self-doubts. To his determination and strength of character was added insecurity after his parents broke up when he was fourteen. Homesick and unhappy at prep and public school until his last year at each, he had similar problems to Christopher at being taken out of his own age group. Like his father, he was in Tonbridge's 1st XI at the age of thirteen. It was a dilemma for the master in charge of cricket as it had been in Colin's time: does a junior boy play in the 1st XI?

Graham felt he did not score enough runs at school, although the record books are only partially in accord. In his last year at Wellesley House he averaged 85 with the bat: his mother was embarrassed by the sheer weight of runs he scored. In his first of five seasons in the Tonbridge 1st XI he batted down the order and bowled leg-breaks. These were later abandoned and by his last year he had switched to military medium, which came to be of occasional benefit to Kent thereafter. As a batsman he was destroying bowling; as captain in 1982 he was aggressive and keen. He did not, it was true, score as heavily as Christopher. Indeed, he scored more runs, 731, in his penultimate year, 1981, than in his last year, 691. He was the better prospect; but Christopher was the more consistent of the two. Just as Christopher endeavoured to bat differently from Colin, so Graham aimed to play differently from Christopher. He developed into a fierce hitter of the ball.

He felt he was pushed into playing professional cricket: 'A schedule was laid out for me and I had arguments with masters at Tonbridge. After I joined Kent I was still questioning myself as to whether it was my decision or made by other people.' Of all the children, he, not blessed with Christopher's out-going disposition, found his surname hardest to bear. It was expected that he should progress in the game – and the expectations, coming as they often did after a goal had been reached, were considerable.

If Graham was pushed into professional cricket, it was not by Colin, who encouraged his sons to play all sports. It remains Graham's biggest disappointment that he never saw Colin play first-class cricket and only on rare occasions did he watch him bat in club matches: he values his technical advice and he has needed it, for he found, like many before him, that after his first season there were few easy runs to be had. If he was pushed into playing cricket, it was not immediately so: he followed Jeremy to Durham University, failed his anthropology exam in his general arts course at the end of his first year and decided, without total conviction, to give County cricket his full attention.

Penny Cowdrey, photographed at her daughter's wedding in 1986.

Chapter Eight

Inevitable Comparisons

O N 1 DECEMBER 1978 the *Daily Mail* carried, on their front page, an exclusive story that Colin Cowdrey had left home after 22 years of marriage. Colin, who had long since retired, had not subsequently been in the public eye; yet the story also occupied the whole of Nigel Dempster's column on an inside page.

The children, who had been told of what was to happen, were stunned less by the fact that their parents had matrimonial difficulties than by what they saw as the enormity of the press coverage. 'It was treated like a soap opera,' said Christopher. He was 21 at the time and still living at home. His youngest brother, Graham, was at school. His housemaster at Tonbridge, David Kemp, cut out all references he could find before the newspapers of the day were handed out to the boys.

For the tabloid papers, as it had been for *Private Eye*, this was a truly gossipy story. Colin, one of England's foremost sportsmen, who had an image of moral rectitude, had left home for, reportedly, his love of Lady Anne Fitzalan-Howard, daughter of the sixteenth Duke of Norfolk. She had first met Colin through her father, who had managed M.C.C.'s 1962–63 tour of Australia. The head of the Roman Catholic church in Britain, he had owned Arundel Castle and its cricket ground, where traditionally touring sides began their itinerary. He liked Colin, admired him as a cricketer and had treated him as if he were his own son.

As the eldest of four daughters of the Duke, who had died in 1975, Lady Anne inherited the only one of his nine titles which could pass to the female line. She became Baroness Herries of Terregles, which dated to 1840, and inherited Everingham Park near York, a large estate. She became joint Master of the Middleton Hunt and a National Hunt trainer. In 1978, at the age of 40, she had returned from Everingham to Arundel, where she was training. Her mother, Lavinia, Duchess of Norfolk, owned stables at Arundel; Lady Anne's own stables were sited close to the isolated house she had built for herself from two cottages at nearby Angmering Park. Determined and devoted to Colin, she was to introduce him to racing: in due course he was to own a horse, where previously he had had a greyhound which ran at homespun Catford.

When a parent leaves home, the natural instincts of the children tend to be protection of the spouse left behind. In addition, they had seen all too little of their father, even when they were not at boarding school. A cricketer's career, with the attendant long absences from home, is not conducive to an easy marriage. Colin himself had foreseen what might arise when he wrote in 1962 in *Time for Reflection*: 'As in every walk of life, there can be a real danger in the husband's travelling and growing in stature, while the wife is left behind without the same opportunities. Homes are often broken this way. Touring means sacrifices which the average cricketer does not always fully appreciate.' Of the children, Jeremy, then aged eighteen, remained both the closest to his father as well as protective towards his mother. More than once he and Christopher had to cope with removing photographers who were laying siege outside her front door. It left him with an abiding distaste of the press. Penny, though, was all too responsive to their telephone calls. The result was a seemingly never-ending series of features, predominantly on the women's pages of tabloid newspapers, the gist being that Penny wanted her husband back and would not agree to a divorce. Hence although she did not oppose the decree, the divorce was not granted until 1985. In September of that year Colin married Lady Anne, quietly, in Sussex. An announcement was placed on the Court and Social page of *The Times*.

Amidst all this, Christopher was trying to shape his career. The senior players of Kent, several of them Test cricketers, were sympathetic, and they also respected him for not trading on his surname. Those who had played with his father treated him as a cricketer in his own right. As for the comparisons, he pre-empted them. 'I shall not mind if I am not as good as my father,' he said, 'so long as I am good enough.' The title of his book, published nine years after his first-class debut, suggested that he was still unsure of the answer. Initially, his self-confidence derived from his good looks; later it was through his cricketing achievements. It was as well he took after his mother. 'If he had a brooding nature,' said Asif Iqbal, Christopher's first County captain, 'he may have found it difficult to overcome the problem of following his father, for people would compare the two, however unnecessary or pointless such a comparison may be.' Similar difficulties had beset Sir Leonard Hutton's son, Richard. 'Tha'll never be as good as thy father,' he would be told bluntly. It is not just the catty spectator who delights in contrasting father and son. It is a game beloved of many cricket followers and journalists, especially if they have seen both play.

In looks, build and gait there are similarities between Colin and Christopher; and in turn between Colin and Graham. Of their characteristics, few are common to all three. And yet Christopher has inherited from his father four notable qualities: kindness to friends, a sense of public relations, a quick wit and, of course, a profound enthusiasm for cricket.

Had Christopher not captained Young England to West Indies in 1976, a party that included David Gower and Mike Gatting, he might well have played in the same Kent XI as his father. As it was, he made his debut in 1977 against the Australians. Two years earlier his father had won the corresponding match for Kent. So there were comparisons aplenty. It was to Christopher's benefit that owing to rain, the steadfast ally of all nerve-wracked cricketers, he did not have to bat. He did, though, take the prized wicket of Doug Walters.

Later that summer Christopher made a century against Glamorgan (which his father never managed) and another in a Benson and Hedges Cup quarter-final. 'Let us have a stiff drink,' Colin said to John Woodcock when he met him that morning, 'for Christopher is down to open.' It was a significant innings for it was made under pressure against a Sussex attack which included John Snow and Tony Greig. Kent had needed 265 to win and Christopher, before he was fully into his stride, had run out his captain. Yet, relieved of making all the running at a crucial stage by Alan Ealham, he pulled and drove to good effect, won the gold award, plaudits from the press – and some prickly comments from Kent members in the bar. 'Your father got a hundred in his first Benson and Hedges match, didn't he?' And then: 'You ought to get runs with your background.'

It would have been unthinkable at the time but it might well have benefited Christopher – and Graham – to have begun their careers with a less fashionable county under the aegis of an old pro. It was almost impossible to escape Colin's capacious shadow. 'I found it harder to play in front of our own crowds than at away grounds,' said Christopher. 'In Kent the spectators always wanted to see how good I was. I couldn't help thinking that some of them felt I was only in the side because of my father. If I was out for nought, people would come up and say, "How did you get a duck with your cricketing background?" If I made a century, they expected it. In other parts of the country I was just one of the opposition. Small things, maybe, but they affect you. It put me back two years, I think.' Possibly he repined overmuch, but he deliberately attempted to play differently from his father. 'At school I played most shots, and straight. Since I left, I've concentrated more on the leg-side. I wanted to avoid the obvious comparisons being made.'

He was fortunate in one sense: he was a cricketer for his time. Strongly built, he was well suited to the limited-overs game. Where Colin had caressed the ball, he cracked it. He was a quicker mover in the field than his father as well as an excellent slip, and had a better throw. There was something of Keith Miller about his movements. As a change bowler who could swing the ball, albeit without proper control, he had the knack of breaking partnerships. Ian Botham was to joke that he was a 'cafeteria bowler'. 'You help yourself to rubbish and then you pay for it!' Unlike Colin, he revelled in slogs and run saving. He responded to crowds – 'there's not the same incentive in championship cricket in front of a handful of people.' Woodcock reckoned when he saw him in that quarter-final at Canterbury that his style was baroque to Colin's classical.

In later years Christopher reckoned that his Benson and Hedges century was the worst thing that could have happened to him. Seven innings of 30 runs apiece might have been more beneficial. His form fell away to the extent that he was left out of Kent's side in the final, a decision which Asif regretted

Christopher, with head gear foreign to his father, ever alert for quick runs. (Associated Sports Photography)

later. Kent lost the match and Grahame Clinton, Christopher's replacement, was out for a duck. Christopher, though, was not one to complain.

Kent were to win the championship in each of Christopher's first two years as a county cricketer, sharing it in 1977 with Middlesex. In a strong side he was often batting down the order and consequently coming in when quick runs were needed, yet still having to concern himself with finishing the season with a decent average. 'It's a very selfish game. I don't enjoy blocking the last few overs when the result is a foregone conclusion but there comes a stage when one can be dropped for hitting twenty and getting out, instead of finishing undefeated on five or six. Committee people don't like that attitude.' He did not find, in the long-term, that he gained from attempting to work the ball to leg, from consciously trying to play in a different way from his father. In County cricket bowlers swiftly become aware of a young batsman's leanings. They learned to bowl on and outside Christopher's off-stump, just as a decade later they were to dig the ball in short of a length at Graham.

Asif and Graham Johnson, two players with whom he had a particular affinity, impressed upon him the need to condition his mind to building large innings. 'I overdid it at first,' he admitted. 'I wanted to be a Botham or a Gower.' He found it hard, too, to adapt after Wellesley House and Tonbridge to batting on wet and indifferent pitches. He was fortunate to be awarded his county cap in 1979 after two seasons averaging 25 and 22: it was to be a further four years before he fully established himself in the side. There were Kent players who half expected to see his name on the unretained list around this time. Six years elapsed between him scoring his first and second centuries in county cricket.

This was not entirely unconnected with his predilection for making the most of what county cricketers call 'the treadmill', the socialising off the field and the varied venues which are a cricketer's lot. Although not a good judge of character, he possessed the common touch with cricketers from different backgrounds. He had a penchant for pubs, was attractive to women and did not take himself too seriously, even when Ken Higgs gave him a vicious bouncer first ball on his initial appearance at Grace Road. 'That was for your father,' said Higgs. Christopher merely laughed.

He also enjoyed gambling. 'We'll make a cricketer out of him,' joked Colin Page, Kent's manager, 'if only we can get him to bed on time.' Mark Nicholas, the Hampshire cricketer and one of his closest friends, felt that Christopher in his bachelor years was 'a natural playboy, mischievous and keen to gamble for a healthy stake. Often was the time that the telephone would ring at midnight and it would be Christopher offering odds against Davis or Higgins as the late-night snooker got underway.'

As Christopher grew older, so he became more ambitious. In 1982, having had his best season to date the previous year, he was appointed joint vice-captain of Kent with Chris Tavaré. Asif, then in his last season, had refused suggestions that he make him Kent's official vice-captain: although he had felt for some time that Christopher would become a competent leader, he viewed it as being too early in his career. Christopher was still predominantly a one-day cricketer – he had yet to score 1,000 runs or take fifteen wickets in a season with his little-used medium pace – and Tavaré, an established Test player and more mature man, was appointed captain for 1983 in succession to Asif. It was a bitter blow to Christopher, who had long wanted to captain Kent: he was made vice-captain but thought seriously about leaving the county. His father, who was on the Kent committee, was instrumental in persuading him to stay. 'Nobody had ever told me before that I wasn't good enough and I sat through a long, depressing week in my flat in Sydney where I was spending the winter playing for Cumberland Cricket Club in Parramatta. But that depressing, thoughtful week was necessary. It was a turning point. I came to realise that the Kent committee was quite correct: I wasn't, on the evidence so far, good enough. I hadn't put in the hard graft on my game. . . . my figures did not suggest I had made the right sort of progress,' he wrote in *Good Enough?*

Christopher worked on his technical flaws, developed his off-side play and tried, that winter, to cut out leg-side shots. His pride had been affected; and he returned to England a more determined cricketer. He was to play his best cricket for Kent during the two years Tavaré captained the side and he did not attempt to usurp power, yet there was a clash of personalities.

140

Christopher the bowler. Control may be lacking, but enthusiasm is not. (Associated Sports Photography)

Captain and vice-captain were the very antithesis of each other: one quiet and analytical, a mentor to younger players, the other a hyperactive, fun-loving extrovert. And their relationship was not helped by Christopher being quizzed by outsiders as to why he had not been made captain. He led the side when Tavaré was playing for England, and with some success. His batting in 1983 was a revelation: he finished seventh in the national averages (1,364 runs, average 56). It was the first time in his career that he had scored 1,000 runs in a season and it was the first time in ten years that a Cowdrey had finished in the leading ten in the averages. A goodish season in 1984 (1,039 runs at 30) culminated in his scoring a half-century in the NatWest final against Middlesex, who won an excellent match off the very last ball. That morning, the gist of several articles was that if he scored a half-century or took five wickets, he had a fair chance of making England's winter tour. As a result of grafting at his game and developing his off-side strokes, Christopher was now a passably orthodox batsman.

One week at the end of the 1984 season was highly significant for him. Before the final, Kent's committee decided to sack Tavaré, who had had a poor season with the bat but had improved Kent's standing in the County championship: they finished in fifth place, having been seventh in 1983, when they also lost in the NatWest final. It was an unexpected decision in that Tavaré, in addition to having brought about a marked improvement in Kent's cricket, was also highly respected by the players. When he had been appointed in 1982 it was only by a narrow head over Christopher. There were members of the committee keen that a Cowdrey should captain Kent: they saw him even then as a possible future captain of England. Early in the season Tavaré had gleaned that his position was in some jeopardy; his outlook became defensive and he did not help his cause with a tediously slow innings for England against Sri Lanka. It was viewed by Kent's committee as uninspiring batting. In the week in which he lost the captaincy of Kent he was omitted for England's party to tour India and Australia — and Christopher included. Not for the first time, a cricketer had clinched his place as a result of a notable performance in the NatWest final, even if that form of the game bore no significance to Test cricket.

It looked at one stage in the autumn of 1984 as if the tour would barely commence. Three hours after England arrived in Delhi, Mrs Gandhi, the Prime Minister, was assassinated. Then, 24 hours before the first Test was due to start, Percy Norris, the deputy High Commissioner in Bombay, was also killed. The England players had been at a function at his house the previous evening; Christopher had taken a liking to his daughter. He was stunned by the mayhem, not least that in India a difference over religion could be a motive for a murder. The uncertainties over whether the tour would go ahead were such that Christopher's selection for the first Test was completely overshadowed. It was a surprising decision: he had played in only one match in which he had scored eight runs and had bowled four overs. Not only was he patently not in form, he was hobbling around with a groin injury. Yet his inclusion, batting at number six, and his worth as a change bowler who had a reputation for taking wickets through sheer variety (which included bad balls) made England a more balanced team in the absence of Ian Botham.

On an easy-paced pitch in the Wankhede Stadium, Bombay, he batted at number six for an hour before he was caught at the wicket off an arm ball from Yadav, an off-spinner. He had made thirteen. On the coach going back to the hotel that evening David Gower, his captain and a close friend, turned to him and said, 'Well, Cow—no-one can take it away from you. It's Kent and England now.' Better was to come. With India in the ascendancy, Christopher was asked by Gower to try to make a breakthrough. With his fourth ball, still wearing his shin pads from having fielded at short leg, he bowled Kapil Dev with a ball that cut back – to this day he knows not how. In London Colin, who never managed to take a Test wicket, was so engrossed in listening to this in the commentary on his car radio that he drove the wrong way up a one-way street. He was flagged down by a policeman just as Christopher broke through. Fortunately, the policeman was a cricket fan; he was let off with a caution.

England lost the match and Christopher had his first experiences of India's pot-pourri of queasy stomachs and dubious umpiring. He was out again to Yadav in the second innings, this time caught at silly point for fourteen. It was an umpiring decision of the kind he had been warned about before the tour started – he did not feel he had hit the ball.

He was left out of the first one-day international but was chosen for the second Test in Delhi. He did not bowl and batted just once as England won by eight wickets. His score of 38, which included two sixes, turned out to be his highest in Test cricket. He was out now through an umpiring verdict that he felt to be not merely dubious but crassly wrong – caught at gully off a boot. He blamed not the umpiring so much as his big feet. At Calcutta, in the third Test, he scored 27 before Yadav had him leg before, and he was wicketless in six overs. At Madras, where England won the fourth Test and the series, he took the all-important wickets of Azharuddin and Kapil Dev, and was undefeated on three when England declared their first innings at 652 for seven. He played in the last two one-day internationals and contributed a single and a wicket to England's cause in the final Test at Kanpur.

In hard statistics, which Christopher has never much liked, he did not have a notable tour – 211 runs at an average of 21 and nine wickets at 49 apiece. His prime contributions had come in less tangible ways: enthusiasm and alacrity in the field, diplomatic endeavour and joie de vivre off it. As ever, he mixed well. His sense of humour was encapsulated by one incident. When Gower asked him if he wanted Gatting to move any wider at slip, he retorted: 'Any wider and he'll burst!' Humour, a vital commodity on any tour of India, was especially important that winter.

Before returning home, England went on to Australia for a series of one-day internationals. Christopher's part in them did not progress beyond the first of these in Melbourne where he played across the line at McDermott to the first ball he received. He was given out lbw, a decision which, on another day, might not have been upheld. In the next match, against Victoria, he broke a hand. His first season as captain of Kent was but seven weeks away.

To cope with captaining Kent, a county which still included several players who had been captained by Colin, and whose dressing-room was split as a result of the dismissal of Tavaré, Christopher had to mature quickly. Tavaré continued to play for Kent, against his will, and kept his own counsel in his corner. He felt that only by concentrating on his own batting could he get through the season. His solitude was not appreciated by those committee members who gained the impression that he was not supportive of Christopher.

Ideally, Christopher would have been better off inheriting the captaincy two years later, when a younger team would have benefited from a style of captaincy that was more extroverted and punchy than that of his predecessor. 'He rides on inspiration and expects his team to ride with him too,' said Mark Nicholas. In 1985 six senior members of the side preferred Tavaré's studious and more disciplined approach, which inevitably made Christopher uncomfortable. It was not the easiest of summers for captain and team, which finished in the middle of the table. Johnson, who was friendly with both parties – he had similar interests to Christopher and had been Tavaré's best man at his wedding – objected strongly to the committee over Tavaré's demotion and after 21 years with the county had his contract terminated for disciplinary reasons before the end of the season. His friendship with Christopher has not been the same since. Graham Dilley, Johnson's brother-in-law, was similarly not enamoured and requested, unsuccessfully, to have his contract cancelled. As Dilley wrote in *Swings and Roundabouts*: 'The situation with Cowdrey was always uneasy because I had made it clear from the start that I was a Tavaré man. Nevertheless, I sought him out, told him how I felt but then added, quite rightly for the good of Kent and its supporters, that despite my feelings I would go out and try my hardest at all times and give the captain my full support. But as the season grew older we began to argue quite often and sometimes heatedly about the way I was getting on and the next thing I knew I was put into the 2nd XI.' Knott, another who preferred Tavaré's style, retired at the end of the season.

Tavaré's dismissal as captain led to insecurity in the dressing room: what, the players wondered, would happen next? As a result, they did not play to their full potential that season. Christopher, inevitably having to feel his way, could not always understand a different viewpoint to his own and was wary of criticism that he was captaining Kent only on account of his surname. His moodiness manifested itself in

145

Christopher catching Graham Roope at Canterbury in 1982. He is an excellent fielder in any position. (The Times *Photo Library)*

disagreements on the field with Nicholas, a friend of long standing: there is nothing Christopher dislikes more than the feeling that he is being mucked around. Their friendship only just survived a major disagreement at Folkestone over a disputed run-out. He vented his feelings to the press and it required the mediation of Richard Ellison, another good friend, to ensure that they made it up at close of play, when Christopher was still seething. It was their second argument of the season, Hampshire having felt that Dilley had resorted to time-wasting tactics in their opening match of the season in April. Their friendship remains nothing if not competitive.

Mark Nicholas was of similar age, background, education and outlook to Christopher. They socialised regularly – which, in spite of their competitiveness, gave cause for concern to the players they led. The Kent and Hampshire sides of that time felt that their relationship was too pally. They disapproved of both captains arriving at the ground together in the morning, unshaven after a night out.

They had mutual friends in London, including two Old Tonbridgians, Tim Wright and Paul Box-Grainger, who had acted once, briefly, as Christopher's agent. He had signed up all of Kent's young players at the start of Christopher's career and had made him a director of the enterprise – which ultimately came unstuck, partly because Christopher was more concerned with playing cricket and with revelry than he was with making money. Nicholas was more self-disciplined. He had no time for the generosity of spirit that Christopher showed towards Wright when captaining Kent against the Australians in 1985. Kent were short of first-team players owing to illness, injury and Johnson's dispute with the club. They were so short of players that they included in their side Brian Luckhurst, then 46 years old and the cricket manager, and made Wright, who was staying with Christopher at his house on the outskirts of Canterbury, the twelfth man. At one point Christopher, who was fielding in the gully, stopped the ball and, as if injured, waved for Wright to come on to the field. As he passed him, Christopher mentioned that he was not badly hurt but was keen to get Wright on; he would return after four overs. It was a timely moment: Wright, a club cricketer, fielded at extra cover with Allan Border, the Australian captain, two runs short of a century. An announcement as to who Wright was came over the tannoy, to applause from Kent members; and he was spared a catch coming his way. It was the kind of gesture an amateur cricketer such as Colin might well have made in an age of less asperity.

Christopher expects, and receives, loyalty from his friends, which he reciprocates. His mother had disapproved of some of the elder company he kept at Tonbridge, which, most probably, had foisted itself upon him. Now, many of his closest friendships were – not surprisingly – with fellow cricketers. With the exception of Kim Barnett, the Derbyshire captain, they were of a type: David Gower, Paul Downton, Nick Kemp and Richard Ellison, all of whom played with or against him for public schools in Kent; and Nicholas, whom he had met in a 2nd XI match in 1977. He was percipient enough to have been wary of the media since his parents split up: he had formed no particular friendships with cricket journalists with the possible exception of Henry Blofeld, who had managed one of three tours he had been on run by Derrick Robins, the millionaire builder. He remained highly sensitive to press criticism, and it worried him that he could not hit it off with Matthew Engel of the *Guardian*, who had been in India. He preferred to keep journalists of all denominations at arm's length. He gave them his time, and courteously; but not his attention.

Christopher will often bounce cricketing ideas off Wright and Box-Grainger. He listens carefully to what Jeremy, his brother, has to say. In his first years as Kent captain he preferred to discuss problems with them rather than with senior players or Luckhurst. Christopher was intent on running his side without a cricket manager, but once Luckhurst was moved sideways and given the nebulous title of cricket administrator, he became depressed at having to deal with complaints from players. Patience was not his strong point; he tended to value a different viewpoint only if he trusted the person concerned. He would rarely lose his temper but Kent's older players recognised in his captaincy a tendency to have similar minor tantrums to his father. He suffered stress more than the ethos of his upbringing would allow him to show; and he did not communicate easily when unsettled, as when he failed to tell Derek Aslett, the bespectacled middle order batsman, that he was not being retained.

Gradually, though, as the older players departed, Christopher began to impose his own positive outlook and flair for ideas upon the club. His invigoration of a younger side was evident in one-day cricket: in 1986 Kent reached the final of the Benson and Hedges Cup, again losing narrowly to Middlesex. In the John Player League they finished joint sixth, compared with joint tenth the year before. In the championship they were again in the middle of the table. That winter they were to lose Dilley, who departed with another swipe at Cowdrey to the effect that even if Tavaré had taken Kent to a string of successes each summer, Christopher would still have been made captain. They were also to lose Terry Alderman, the highly skilled Australian, whose comments on the club had not endeared him to committee members or Christopher. He and Dilley had taken 142 championship wickets between them in 1986. Described by Underwood as 'the best Kent bowler I have seen', he took 98 wickets in nineteen championship matches, yet Christopher still felt concerned about his fitness and that he did not dismiss tail-enders quickly enough. Christopher favoured a faster bowler, one who could trade bouncer for bouncer. When, at the end of the 1986 season, Alderman was asked by a member of the committee what was afflicting Kent's cricket, his reply was unequivocal. 'You've got the wrong captain,' he said. Unsurprisingly, he was not invited back.

Christopher's own form had been patchy after reaching 1,000 runs in 1985 and making his career-best score of 159 against Surrey. In 21 championship matches in 1986 he made just 820 runs. Had Christopher won one of the three one-day finals they had contested in four years it would, as Christopher said, have done much for Kent's confidence. As it was, when Graham played his first match for Kent under his brother's captaincy against the Sri Lankans in 1984, Kent had not won a trophy for six years.

Graham batted once in that match, making seven. He was selected also to play for Young England against Young Australia and was given a foretaste of what to expect. After a second failure at Trent Bridge a Nottinghamshire member exclaimed as he made his way back up the pavilion steps, 'He's only here because he's a bloody Cowdrey!' Like Christopher, he was level-headed enough to realise that he would not be as good as his father; but, judging from the Kent 2nd XI record he set in 1985, he clearly had a talent. He made 1,300 runs in 26 innings and was given his championship debut at Swansea, where he scored 29 against Glamorgan. There followed half-centuries against the Australians and Worcestershire, batting at number six and eight respectively. In five championship matches he scored 187 runs at 37 an innings: only Neil Taylor finished the season with a higher average. Shorter than Christopher, and stockier, his runs were shovelled rather than scored, with plenty of bottom hand brought to bear. Once he got his eye in – his father always told him to play through the 'V' between mid-off and mid-on for the first ten overs – he gave the ball a fearful crack. It was the same with golf. Mark Nicholas described him as 'an awesome striker of the ball'. Like Christopher, he allied physical strength with a natural sense of timing.

Christopher was particularly anxious that he should not be seen to be favouring Graham: if it was a choice between se-lecting him or a player of equal ability, Christopher would lean towards the latter in attempting to be fair. There were times

149

when Graham felt he should have been chosen earlier than he was in 1985. He was not especially close to Christopher, but he did have considerable respect for him as player and captain. 'Christopher never has to ask me to pull my weight, and he gave me advice on how to play one-day cricket.' Their relationship was by necessity more formal during the summer than the winter: fraternal relations are worthless if the captain is left stranded in mid-pitch as the asking rate mounts at Weston-super-Mare. They were tested when Graham, seemingly peeved at not having had more first-team matches, was widely quoted as saying he was seeking to move to another county. He maintained that he had said he would consider leaving Kent if he was not chosen within the next two years. At the same time he wanted to leave The Mote, the cricket club which played at Mote Park, Maidstone, and join St Lawrence and Highland Court at Canterbury. His request for a guaranteed place in the side had not been granted.

Graham has not been one to set himself specific targets as a cricketer, but he did have one particular ambition: to play an entire season with Kent. After spending the winter of 1985 in Sydney, he played in fifteen of Kent's 24 championship matches in 1986, without conspicuous success after scoring 75 in the first match at Canterbury against Northamptonshire. His finest performances were reserved for the Benson and Hedges Cup: as Christopher had, he was developing an aptitude for one-day cricket. In the zonal rounds he made 65 against Surrey, an unbeaten 60 against Hampshire which won him the gold award from the adjudicator, Sir Leonard Hutton, 34 off Derbyshire in the quarter-finals (adding 56 in seven overs with Christopher) and in the final, a courageous 58 in rain and gloaming against a markedly strong Middlesex attack. Hutton had been especially impressed with his temperament, likening it to that of his father – 'Temperament is so important, you see' – but wondered if he had the stomach for the aggression in the game. In particular, Hutton doubted whether cricket was as enjoyable to play as it had been when Colin was in his prime – 'and he may not like that.'

By the middle of 1986, Graham felt drained. His was a dilemma shared with other talented young batsmen, and which was gradually affecting English cricket. Batting in the middle of

Graham in his first full season for Kent, 1986. Quick runs were always the priority. (Mark Leech)

the order, he was forever having to improvise in the quest for runs, bonus points, myriad one-day trophies. His father, at the start of an innings or approaching a century, had rarely had to recourse to anything so ungainly. 'I rang him up,' said Graham, 'after I struggled on some poor pitches. He told me that when he was going through a bad patch he would look for five runs, then look for ten, and play as straight as possible. The more I played, the more I valued everything he had to say. But he would never telephone me and tell me that such and such a shot was awful.'

In fact, Graham saw all too little of him, or friends from school or university. He found, like many before him, that the transition from 2nd XI to County cricket was harder than anticipated, and that the travelling as a County cricketer was excessive. And as one who had had Christian convictions since he had been at Durham, he disliked having to be in a different place each Sunday. In the winter of 1985–86 he had been on a Christians in Sport tour to India which included Jack Bond, the former Lancashire captain, and Vic Marks, the Somerset and England off-spinner. It was led by Andrew Wingfield Digby, once an Oxford Blue, who gave Graham 'a spiritual injection' every fortnight. The tour had been fulfilling and had strengthened Graham's convictions. They had played strong opposition and had church and prayer meetings in the evenings. And he prayed at the top of the pavilion steps each time he went out to bat.

There was a Christians in Sport movement in Canterbury, which met once a month; but Graham missed, in particular, the guidance of Marks. 'If I could go to church every Sunday with Vic, it would be different,' he said. Nor did he find compensation in the drinking and incessant cricket talk after a day's play that were a cricketer's lot; and he disliked the interference with his reading. With so much travelling and playing, he felt exhausted most evenings. But Derek Underwood stressed the importance of staying for one drink after close of play, that socialising was an aspect of the game and that it was imperative to relax. 'It is very important to enjoy the company of other players, through whom one can learn about the game, and not to keep one's frustrations from the day's play bottled up,' he said. But Graham often preferred to melt away; and the Kent players referred to him as 'Harry Houdini'.

Graham was honest and open about his difficulties: 'I struggled with the contradictions inherent in dressing-room life, the swearing and the pornography. I would have liked to have seen every county having its own chaplain. It was one of my main aims in cricket.' He doubted, in 1986, whether he would still be in the game ten years hence. He was not so much indecisive as undecided. Burdened by his surname, he found it hard to express his gifts, and built a cocoon around himself.

And yet, after his half-century in the Benson and Hedges final, there were critics and, no doubt, spectators suggesting Graham was on the verge of becoming an England batsman. He had adapted well to the one-day game and was not afraid to make room and strike medium-pacers over extra cover or, off the back foot, cut them backward of point; and a high proportion of his runs came from these shots. Although chunkier than Christopher, he was quick between the wickets and in the covers. A nervous tic told of his struggles at the crease, but he did not lack for resolution. It was soon evident, though, that he was not yet ready for England; Underwood, for one, was irritated the subject had ever been mooted. He knew how much Graham still had to learn. In spite of considerable help from Tavaré, his technique was far from perfect; and, of course, he had simply not scored enough runs.

Bald statistics, by which no Cowdrey held great store, indicated that in 1987 Graham's game had come on. From having finished 200th in the national batting averages in 1986, making just 353 runs in fifteen innings, he came exactly 100 places higher that summer, averaging 31 an innings. His was a higher placing than Botham, Amiss, Fletcher – and big brother. The reality was rather different. Bowlers were working out his weaknesses and fastening on to them. Word went round the County circuit that he was vulnerable against short-pitched bowling and consequently he received a good deal of it. He played in just five first-class matches before he had his jaw broken by Michael Holding, who was now playing for Derbyshire. His vulnerability had shown on occasion when he seemingly froze and let himself be hit; now, against Holding, he ducked into a ball that did not get up. Mike Denness, who had

Colin stumped by Taber playing for Old England against Old Australia at the Oval in 1980. Judging by his expression, he will have no need to look at the umpire. (Sport and General)

joined Kent's committee, was concerned that young batsmen, weighed down with their protective panoply, had lost not just the art of weaving out of the line of the short-pitched ball but the adrenalin that flowed from facing fast bowling without protection.

It took five weeks for Graham's injuries to heal. By the time he resumed playing, protected now by a visor attached to his helmet, there was only his place in the side to play for. Without Alderman and Dilley, Kent finished fourteenth in the championship and other than reaching the Benson and Hedges semi-finals, made little impression in the one-day game. It was at the end of the 1987 season that Aslett was released and, since he and Graham were effectively competing for the same place in the batting order, it was surmised that this was for expedience. The committee's view was that Aslett had achieved all he was going to achieve; that, rising 30, he would not improve further. Graham was awarded his county cap

154

during the season, which, since it was questionable whether it had been merited by his performances, owed considerably to the committee's evaluation of his potential – and, the cynics put it, to his family.

Mark Nicholas reckoned that Graham would give anything to become a really successful batsman. He was prepared to theorise about batting in a way that was foreign to Christopher, and it took great courage to hook Holding over the square-leg boundary when, as inevitably happened, he was not spared short-pitched bowling on their first meeting after Graham's injury. When Kent beat Derbyshire that afternoon in a Sunday match at Chesterfield, Graham was still at the wicket, having reached a notable half-century.

Christopher, meanwhile, had had a season in 1987 which approximated with expectations and achievements: as near to 1,000 runs as made little difference; an average of 30 which mirrored that over his career; nineteen wickets; and his most consistent batting coming in the one-day game. Of greater concern was Kent's record under his leadership. In three seasons they had not won a trophy and had not fared as consistently as in the two seasons when Tavaré, albeit with a stronger side, was captain. On BBC TV's 'Maestro', Colin had said in 1985 that if Christopher had not won a trophy two years hence, he knew the score: he would be dismissed. It had been a different matter, Colin said, in his time; now, no County committee was prepared to wait for success.

Yet Christopher's tenure seemed secure. He had, as Johnson put it, 'a strong power base' on the committee, including, of course, his father, who had resigned from the executive committee after Christopher had been appointed captain. Although Tavaré remained on Kent's staff and was to do so until his four-year contract and benefit were completed in 1988, he was most unlikely to be re-instated as captain. Neither was there any one person on the staff considered of sufficient merit to captain Kent at a future date; except, that is, Graham.

Chapter Nine

The Game Administrator

ICHAEL COLIN COWDREY was barely born when his father wrote from India to two friends in England asking them to put him down for M.C.C. membership. He never did discover whether that was the inspiration behind giving him the famous initials. It was as if his father was already looking to the day when his only son would preside over the most famous cricket club in the world.

It was an apposite choice, then, when Jack Davies, the out-going President, nominated Colin to be his successor for M.C.C.'s bicentenary year, 1987. Colin cared deeply for the club, its traditions and its future. He knew that many, including eminent individuals, were questioning M.C.C.'s role in the modern game given that it had ceded responsibility for the running of cricket in England to the Test and County Cricket Board in 1968. Did the private club still have a function? He was disturbed, too, at a deterioration in relations between the two bodies, both of which he had served. His had to be the authoritative voice in defining the *raison d'être* for M.C.C.'s existence.

One of the drawbacks of being President is that office is held for just one year. Hence the incoming President relies heavily on the secretariat. There is only so much impact he can make on the affairs of both the club and the International Cricket Conference (now the International Cricket Council). Until the I.C.C.'s constitution was changed in 1989, the President of M.C.C. automatically chaired its annual meeting. Nonetheless, Colin said he had high hopes when he was appointed, hopes that included encouraging the development of facilities at Lord's, which M.C.C. owned; restoring a balance between bat and ball, even if it meant altering the composition of the ball to make it softer and

drawing a line down the middle of the pitch to reduce intimidatory bowling. Here, there were possibilities. Other than owning
Lord's, M.C.C.'s most prized possessions are their reputation,
and their responsibility for drawing up the laws of the game.

Colin was always, he said, keen to maximise the independence of M.C.C. 'For 200 years we have been concerned with the
balance between bat and ball. When Sir Donald Bradman felt
strongly about introducing eight-ball overs, M.C.C. were quick
to give it a try. Now we are concerned about short-pitched
bowling, how to help the spinner back into the game and slow
over-rates. We want to see intimidatory bowling arrested. I am
keen to reach out to each M.C.C. member and remind him
to watch over these aspects in his local club or school. One
can see intimidatory bowling appearing even at those levels of
cricket.'

Colin conceded that arresting intimidatory bowling, as he
put it, would be unlikely to come about before the end of
his year in office. Indeed, the issue was still afflicting Test
cricket when he took on the chairmanship of the I.C.C. for
a second spell three years later. This was a laudable ambition
but, as with other of his enthusiasms, he would find it hard to
follow it through.

A more realisable project was the continuation of work
already underway to upgrade Lord's. He saw this as his priority.
'No-one can be happy with an arena this size left empty for
seven months of the year. Although meetings are held there
every day and the cricket school is packed out, the ground is
probably only full for six days of the year. That is disturbing.
By the year 2000 we want to have brought Lord's up to a high
standard,' he said. M.C.C. had already embarked on building
the new Mound Stand, owing to the generosity of Paul Getty,
who had contributed £2m. M.C.C. had long been looking into
the possibility of building at the Nursery End, although they
were handicapped by the railway line which went directly
underneath. Three years later M.C.C. were to embark on
work there, although it was to be on the seating rather than
the actual Nursery ground, where the nets were still sited.

Colin saw the Presidency of M.C.C. in its bicentenary year as
the pinnacle of his career. His signature now bore the hallmark
of his position: M. Colin Cowdrey. He was planning to preside

157

over a series of glittering celebrations ranging from dinners in the Long Room to a banquet at Guildhall on the eve of the special fixture in August between M.C.C. and Rest of the World, and the commemoration of M.C.C.'s first match, against Essex in 1787. He wanted, understandably, to ensure that the celebrations were not blighted by any contentious issues. He had also, according to Raman Subba Row, his old friend and chairman of the T.C.C.B., grown more decisive with age.

Before Colin took up his year in office in October 1986, he called an informal meeting at Barclays of representatives from I.C.C. countries. Allan Rae, then President of West Indies Cricket Board of Control, had been especially concerned about the future of international cricket following England's turbulent tour of West Indies earlier that year, their heavy defeats and the controversies off the field. He did not want such a tour repeated. Colin's initiative led to the forming of an I.C.C. select committee made up of individuals from each member country plus three associate members and himself as chairman. In addition to the considerable work involved in planning and executing the bicentenary celebrations, Colin was charged with directing discussions to avert a split as a result of a West Indies motion to exclude from Test cricket anyone playing or coaching in South Africa, whether as an individual or as part of a team. The World Cup, scheduled for 1987, was also threatened by India's objections to players with South African connections. At the first of two I.C.C. meetings during the summer, some of his difficulties were postponed. The select committee would be set up with the intention of reporting back the following year.

By nature good at consulting – which, if overdone, can lead to a charge of indecisiveness – and listening, Colin was also an emollient figure in that his attempts at mediating in the D'Oliveira affair and his speech at Central Hall, Westminster, in 1983, opposing sending an M.C.C. side to the Republic, were well known. He continued to make it clear that M.C.C. would not contemplate changing their stance.

His preoccupations, though, were mostly closer to home. He had been disappointed, originally, that M.C.C. had had to give way to the T.C.C.B. in some respects in the modernisation of cricket in 1968. 'Somehow I am a little sad about the changes. I view it all with some misgiving, and wonder whether the commercial conglomerate into which it appears to be developing can ever have quite the same family touch again,' he wrote. The decisiveness to which Subba Row was referring was especially evident in his desire to tackle the growing conflicts between M.C.C. and the T.C.C.B., both of which were camped at Lord's, before the bicentenary season began. Subba Row said, and it can rarely have been said of Colin before: 'He bit the bullet.' Of all the more recent Presidents of M.C.C., he was seemingly the least likely to take any decisive measures.

A report initiated by Subba Row almost a decade prior to 1986 had recommended the virtual demise of M.C.C.'s wider role. The T.C.C.B. attained more power when, in 1982, they gained authority by their dominance of the Cricket Council to run all aspects of cricket in England. They remained, however, mere tenants at Lord's, from which they derived a large proportion of their income through Test matches staged there; and they were a fledgling organisation by comparison with M.C.C. Subba Row found, in Jack Bailey, a trenchant secretary of M.C.C. who, far from prepared to accept its decline in power at Lord's, zealously guarded its hegemony. Then 56, a former Oxford captain and County cricketer 'and a strong-willed and competent individual, he had been profoundly affected by the findings in the dispute between the T.C.C.B. and World Series Cricket. He felt that M.C.C. should, at all costs, retain control of Lord's. He was seemingly well-established, in that he had been secretary since 1974; he counted himself, too, as a friend of both Colin and Subba Row.

The kernel of the issue was that the T.C.C.B. felt it should have absolute control over those who ran matches at Lord's. M.C.C., while ceding responsibility to the T.C.C.B., maintained that they should continue to have control of the ground. The upshot, Tony Lewis wrote in his book on M.C.C., *Double Century*, was that 'M.C.C. is accused of fortress politics and the secretariat seen as jealous of the low ground of power.' By the time the book was published, in what should have been a celebratory summer, the matter had come to a head.

Bailey was keen that M.C.C. should not give jurisdiction of Lord's to the T.C.C.B., even though he soon discovered that Colin, the in-coming President, was clearly backing Subba Row. Bailey reckoned he smelled a conspiracy.

Colin could be easily bored by minutiae or financial details, but he was clearly surprised that Bailey was prepared stubbornly to maintain his ground in the face of considerable pressure and discomfort both to himself and to Colin. Whatever occurred, M.C.C.'s committee did not want the issue brought out into the open, although legal advice had been obtained advocating they consult the membership.

In October of 1986, the month in which Colin began his term in office, Bailey went on holiday. When he returned he said that he found that Colin and Sir Anthony Tuke, a former President, were running M.C.C.'s affairs. Bailey was excluded by Colin from an M.C.C. meeting discussing the T.C.C.B. later that month and came to the conclusion, finally, that the only option was for him to resign forthwith. Colin was not the first President of M.C.C. to conclude that Bailey's resistance to the T.C.C.B.'s ambitions at Lord's had meant that there were difficulties between English cricket's foremost bodies – Charles Palmer, who had been both a President of M.C.C. and chairman of T.C.C.B. was prepared to back him publicly – and yet, supported by a substantial majority on M.C.C.'s committee, Colin had been the only one prepared to fall in with the T.C.C.B.'s wishes. He had done so, summarised an editorial in *The Cricketer*, 'with a toughness he was not supposed to have had as a player.' He was also supposed to be temperamentally slow to make up his mind. Bailey was inevitably critical of Colin in his subsequent book, *Conflicts in Cricket* – but not as critical as he would have been had not his lawyers read the relevant pages first.

In due course the issue surfaced in the press, not least in the *Sunday Telegraph*, which published an article based on an interview with David Clark, M.C.C.'s treasurer and Colin's former captain, who resigned in sympathy with Bailey. It was strongly dismissive of a letter Colin sent to the club's 18,000 members in an attempt to explain Bailey's early retirement. Colin wrote to the effect that there would have been a complete breakdown in relations between M.C.C. and the T.C.C.B. had the secretary remained. The *Sunday Telegraph* revealed that M.C.C.'s solicitors were unhappy both with the letter and the contents of the annual report. They refused to endorse part of the report and accounts. The articles by John Reason focused on the T.C.C.B.'s attempts to exert their domain over matches at Lord's and over their share of members' facilities there. He wrote that M.C.C.'s committee had received legal advice that they should report to the club's membership before accepting the T.C.C.B.'s demands, and that they had not done so.

Clark's concerns were primarily that M.C.C.'s committee had not supported him in his belief that members of the club should be consulted before any change was agreed with the T.C.C.B. relating to control of major matches at Lord's, and that legal advice sought by the committee had been ignored. He also was perturbed by the committee's 'method' of enforcing Bailey's retirement. 'To bow to pressure from an outside body [the T.C.C.B.] seemed to me to lack loyalty to the club's chief executive [Bailey] and to lower the standards of integrity which I have always associated with M.C.C.,' he said. He questioned why Bailey had not been given a subscription list for contributions from members, as was customary on the retirement of long-serving officers of M.C.C. Clark felt, too, that the committee and members had to resolve the problems of conflict of interest arising from dual membership of the committees of M.C.C. and the T.C.C.B. His belief that M.C.C. members should be properly consulted did strike a chord with the committee: in due course M.C.C. appointed a public relations firm to keep its membership, and the outside world, better informed.

On 6 May, the M.C.C. report and accounts were not accepted at the club's annual general meeting. It was a crowded and heated affair, and those present at Lord's were not prepared to accept the committee's decision to affirm the T.C.C.B.'s ultimate responsibility for matches there. The attendance was double the normal turn-out for an A.G.M. One speaker, Freddie Millett, a former captain of Cheshire, claimed that 'a weak committee had given way to T.C.C.B. blackmail' with reference to an alleged threat to take Test matches away from Lord's.

It was the first time in M.C.C.'s 200-year history that the report and accounts were not adopted. Colin was incredulous, putting the motion to adopt a second time. This had no effect: the committee were fortunate to escape a vote of no confidence and Colin decided that the meeting would have to be reconvened. The business of the day was not fully completed and instead of resuming the business of the A.G.M., a special meeting was convened. As ever, Colin put on a brave smile, pleased at least that he had avoided further embarrassment. In a sense he was playing for time. The business which remained unfinished included a proposal by Millett that sought some assurances as to the way M.C.C. was run in future.

The time that Colin obtained was put to effect. M.C.C. dispensed with the services of their solicitors of long standing, Halsey, Lightly and Hemsley. A special general meeting was called for 30 July, the recalcitrant members, criticised in some quarters as a faction, were kept at arm's length and the report and accounts accepted by 7,138 votes to 981. The poll was conducted through postal as well as personal votes, which the committee felt bound to implement seeing as the outcome was of vital importance to the club. They were reassured by an 80 per cent majority among those who cast their votes at the meeting. Bailey felt the committee had designated only those aspects that they wanted discussed but was well aware that the well-being of the club was ultimately of overriding importance.

When the special meeting took place, Colin was not present. He was seriously ill, recovering from a heart by-pass operation. Hubert Doggart, the newly-appointed treasurer, presided over the meeting, the banquet at Guildhall and the bicentenary match itself. Doubtless the exertions of the preceding months had adversely affected Colin's health: it was a dreadful disappointment for him not to enjoy the fruits of labours long planned with Doggart. He sent a message to the banquet: 'Keep cricket a happy game.'

In his absence, his determination to come to grips with short-pitched bowling had come to naught. The United Kingdom's proposal, put forward to the main meeting of the I.C.C. in August, was that a bowler be limited to just one bouncer per over. If he bowled a second the umpire would no-ball and warn him, and inform the fielding captain and his fellow umpire.

*The President of M.C.C. wears an I. Zingari blazer and an early pill box cap. He is holding a mid-18th-century oak bat. The event is an auction of memorabilia in M.C.C.'s bicentenary year. (*The Times *Photo Library)*

163

If the offence was repeated, the bowler would be debarred from bowling for the remainder of the innings. A bouncer was defined as a ball passing over the shoulder of a batsman standing upright. The proposal was unique in that it allowed for only one warning rather than the uniform two.

The I.C.C. has often been accused of having 'no teeth', although Colin saw that there were advantages in this owing to the growing pressure of political restraints. They chose, at any rate, not to accept this proposal nor another that bowlers' run-ups should be limited to 30 yards. Not surprisingly, West Indian arguments prevailed against the limitation of one bouncer per over.

Colin and others, all too aware of indulgent standpoints, had been of the thinking that the chairman of I.C.C. should now be in office for two years, which would give him greater opportunity for tackling contentious issues. It was felt that a former cricketer rather than a public figure such as, say, Sir Anthony Tuke, should cope with increasingly complex cricketing matters.

It says much for his unquenchable enthusiasm for cricket that two years later Colin was keen to take on the chairmanship of I.C.C. again. The on-the-field issues he faced when President of M.C.C. (the two posts were no longer connected) had not been resolved: problematical umpiring, bouncers, a dearth of spin, were familiar topics. He deplored the trend towards more and more protection for batsmen – he himself felt that his movements would have been restricted had he worn a helmet. His theory that the ball should be softer still pertained: only a batsman with a reputation as a courageous player of fast bowling could have suggested that, and written that the earliest cricketers made a serious mistake when they played the game with a hard ball.

'I have taken so many knocks myself that I shall carry them with me into old age,' he wrote in *The Lord's Taverners Sticky Wicket Book*. 'It was a tragic mistake not to have a soft ball. My complaint is that the helmet should not really have to come into play. That it does so, and is necessary, concedes that there is too much rough intent. The administrators have been slow to act, mainly because they have found it so difficult to frame a law which defines a bouncer. It is cricket as a game of skills that we must seek to promote and preserve.' He apportioned some of the blame to World Series Cricket – 'to the cricket connoisseur it has been hard to take' – and added that he was glad the players involved had not enjoyed it.

Then there was the perennial problem of South Africa. For Christopher to join the unofficial England party to play there in 1990 and 1991 was embarrassing enough; for Colin would be left to pick up the pieces. Just before the first of these tours began, a number of former England captains, including Peter May, wrote to *The Times* suggesting that I.C.C. send a working party there to investigate the changes that the South African Cricket Union had wrought. May, who had been to South Africa the previous year, had informed Colin of this in advance; but Colin had no immediate plans to take up the idea, not least because England's official tour of West Indies was imminent, as indeed was his own visit there.

The new constitution of I.C.C. having been agreed, with a change of name, Colin, as its first chairman, was to serve a maximum period of four years. It would take him to the eve of his 61st birthday. He was, as he approached the age of 60, winding down his business commitments. As with his contemporaries, May and Dexter, he was fortunate in that his work did not preclude him from his multifarious cricket commitments; and he was able to put back into the game as much as he had taken out. He retired officially from Barclays in February 1988, having been an advisory local director of the south east region. He was retained as a consultant for 100 days a year thereafter, and continued to maintain an office, and his own personal assistant, at their City of London headquarters.

Living as he was at Angmering Park, a few miles from Arundel, Colin was playing an increasingly prominent part in the running and the development of the game at one of England's most charming grounds. For Colin it was the perfect backdrop, just as Canterbury and Lord's had been throughout his years as a first-class cricketer. He had long savoured playing at Arundel, with its blend of grandeur and bonhomie; and when the 16th Duke of Norfolk, his manager on M.C.C.'s tour of Australia in 1962–63, died in 1975, Colin assisted in forming the Arundel Castle Cricket Club. He launched the appeal which led to its formation. On the death of the Duke, the title had passed to a cousin, a soldier of 60 who had negligible interest in the game. Hence Colin's expertise was vital. 'Cricket cannot continue at Arundel without a club to support it,' he said. He became its vice-chairman.

This was also the year in which Colin retired from first-class cricket. Now he was able to play at Arundel more often; and three years later, when he left Penny and went in due course to live in the vicinity, he could provide further impetus. He would always appear at the traditional early-season match between Lavinia, Duchess of Norfolk's XI and the touring side. He would be the one person the tourists would know of and want to meet: it was as if, when he shook hands, a royal personage had arrived. Of the individuals who guided cricket after the Duke's death, he had a greater impact and range of contacts than even Ronnie Aird and Billy Griffith, both former secretaries of M.C.C. The Duchess gave him considerable support; so, too, did Eddie Harrison, the secretary of Sussex Martlets, who played at the ground.

Colin became, in addition, one of five trustees of Arundel Castle Cricket Foundation when it was formed, as a charity, in 1986. Its aim was 'to encourage and enhance the education of young people through cricket and cricket instruction at Arundel and elsewhere'. Colin felt the game there needed an uplift, and that the way to achieve it was to make more use of the ground and the castle. With his knowledge of cricket and the financial expertise of the chairman, Roger Gibbs, they set out plans to build a cricket centre and to benefit clubs and schools with poor facilities in the south of England. Again, Paul Getty provided backing, enabling an indoor cricket school to be built behind the pavilion and finished, rather later than originally anticipated, in 1989. As a charitable project, no-one was required to pay for the use of the nets, video, a bowling machine and other equipment. Courses were arranged to guide teachers on how best to introduce cricket to their pupils, and coaching sessions were held on school premises, making use of playgrounds and sports halls.

Colin approached John Barclay, then captain of Sussex, to become director of cricket and coaching. An Old Etonian, Barclay was coming towards the end of a worthy career that was being affected by injury; but he retained an enthusiasm for the game that was essential for his task. After retiring he discovered for himself the problems of P.E. teachers at state schools who shied away from instruction at an art in which they were not proficient. Industrial action did not help. Many of the youngsters who came to Arundel had no experience of proper cricket, coaching or equipment.

Barclay saw an opportunity to motivate schools as well as the youngsters themselves and was especially struck by Colin's intense enthusiasm for cricket. 'Many of the cricketers I played with don't have that ingrained love of the game,' he said. Colin happily left fixture planning at Arundel to Barclay, who organises around 40 matches a year there. Colin, who seconded Barclay for election to M.C.C.'s committee, continued to attend as many trustee and committee meetings as he could at Arundel. He still plays the occasional match there, his cricket not so much hampered by operation or recuperation as by advancing years. The Arundel cricket school was officially opened in 1990.

After recovering from his operation, and with his year as President of M.C.C. having ended in the autumn of 1987, Colin turned his attention to affairs at Kent. They had had a poor season. It was the ninth year in succession in which they had not won any of the four trophies and, not surprisingly, there was concern as to the organisation of the club. The committee were uncertain as to whether to employ a coach or a manager, having moved Brian Luckhurst into an administrative role. Moreover, they were unsure as to whether to have a cricket sub-committee. Colin, undeterred by having two sons on the staff, volunteered to the chairman, Major Martin ffrench Blake, to look into the affairs of the club. Though he had resigned from the executive committee when Christopher became captain, he remained on the general committee as one of the four trustees of the club. The trustees were, in effect, watchdogs on behalf of the members with powers to call a special general meeting.

The executive committee was in agreement that Colin should chair a small working party which would include Jim

Woodhouse, a former 2nd XI player whose assertive nature would give rise to strained relations when after becoming at Colin's behest chairman of the cricket committee, he was appointed chief executive of the club. Luckhurst was to guide Colin in his deliberations. This working party was to be a think tank, an *ad hoc* committee with power to recommend rather than to vote; and its brief was to discuss cricketing problems as well as the structure of the club itself. Under Colin it met frequently at first but less often two years later, when discussions had not been made public. Colin had not intended them to be.

As an administrator Colin prefers lobbying out of committee to thrashing out minutiae around a table. He likes to gather individuals or small groups about him, be it after dinners, at Barclays, his St James club (Boodles), or even at Wimbledon. In committee he can appear tired and bored with financial details; outside of it he is persuasive and compelling. He is respected for his cricketing knowledge and gives of his time freely; he is the social equal of fellow committee members; and his covert influence is immense.

Chapter Ten

King for a Day

C HRISTOPHER'S FRIENDS would say that his overriding quality, his prime gift, is his enthusiasm. This extends beyond the boundary and manifests itself in hyperactive ventures and pursuits. Not for him repose in the pavilion on a rainy day: he always wants to be on the field. Failing that, he will be involved in some other game. It is a prized asset, not least when it comes to motivating lethargic cricketers. Decisive, confident and prepared to gamble, Christopher also excelled at the art of mastering press conferences with an articulation that belied his academic results. He was asked a rambling question at Kent's pre-season press day in 1988 to the effect that, with three former captains involved in the administration of the county's affairs – his father, Denness and Ealham – might not his own position be endangered. In a trice he answered, 'You mean they are thinking of making a comeback?' He was as adept at evading a question as his father was at switching it. Both were scored for tact; but Christopher was considerably less circumspect.

By 1988 Kent had not won a trophy for a decade. Their staff was considered to be about the weakest they had had since Christopher's father and Ames had begun to make necessary changes three decades before. Underwood had retired; Eldine Baptiste, the West Indian all-rounder, had been replaced as overseas player by Hartley Alleyne, an esoteric choice since his career with Worcestershire had not been a conspicuous success; Tavaré was not thought to be the batsman he once was. It was no surprise, then, when the first three championship matches were lost, including one against Essex in which Graham made his maiden century. There was a record number of runs, 1,570, scored in this, one of the first of the experimental four-day matches, played on a Chelmsford pitch that was almost too perfect. Graham's innings of 145 was made after he had come in at number seven, and at a stage when Kent were in some difficulties.

Jim Woodhouse, the new chairman of the cricket committee, subsequently held an inquiry in the form of a team meeting at which two vital decisions were taken. The first was to attempt to compensate for the team's shortcomings by concentrating on their fielding, and the second, equally significant, was to appoint John Inverarity, the former Australian Test cricketer, as cricket adviser. Designated to be a headmaster, he had briefly taught at Tonbridge (after Christopher left) and had the teacher's ability to impart information, coupled with extensive knowledge of the game. Christopher trusted him and felt able to communicate with him.

That meeting, and its aftermath, were reminiscent of Kent's championship-winning season of 1970. Now, as then, they had reached their nadir; and improvement was rapidly forthcoming. At the end of May Kent beat Yorkshire, the first of six championship victories in succession. Bowlers hitherto scarcely known took a stack of wickets; batsmen emerged from their carapaces and scored positively. The catches went to hand and Kent went to the top of the table. Christopher was to the fore: always at his best when attacking, his captaincy won matches which might otherwise have been left drawn. Against Nottinghamshire he steered Kent to victory with one ball to spare, scoring ten off four balls in the final over; he made 49 as Kent reached a target of 270 left them by Glamorgan; he made runs and took middle-order wickets as they won both their matches in Tunbridge Wells week, against Middlesex and Lancashire. Warwickshire were beaten by an innings. The credit for Kent's success went to him.

It was now his side in the sense that several of the young players had known no other Kent captain. These included Roy Pienaar, a South African all-rounder who had joined the county almost by accident the previous season when injuries had abounded. He had a keen appreciation of Christopher as both man and captain and was a cricketer of some class. It soon told: Alleyne, who had been injured, could not regain his place. The club was also better run than it had been for a while. Woodhouse, whom Christopher liked, was a sufficiently strong and independent character to provide an effective link between the committee and the players, who were able to speak their mind to him in private. The club continued to be backed by Jeremy's City firm of stockbrokers, James Capel, whose sponsorship of Kent, started in 1986, was worth a minimum of £30,000 a year. Kent were to have been backed by a fruit packing company in the north of England. When they pulled out of the deal, Jeremy informed his chairman, Peter Quinnen, who as a sports enthusiast agreed at once to support the county.

From the middle of June, Kent were never out of the limelight, even though they were not excelling at the one-day game. In marked contrast to this success, England were being thrashed yet again by West Indies and were running through their captains at an alarming rate. Mike Gatting was removed after the first Test and an alleged nocturnal relationship with a barmaid. John Emburey, whose place in the side was in some doubt, was dropped after losing the second and third Tests of the series. The selectors, comprising Peter May, Mickey Stewart, Fred Titmus and Phil Sharpe, met several times to discuss the captaincy after the third Test, only to delay their decision. It was evident that their choice, when announced, was not a unanimous one. 'Not many decisions are,' May said later.

He took a gamble. 'We believe Christopher's style of leadership is what is now required,' he said. He was adamant that a fresh start had to be made, overriding objections from Stewart in particular. There was no embarrassment so far as he was concerned in appointing his godson. 'That was an excuse for other people to use.' In the main, it was well received. Christopher joked about May having doled out his loose change to him when he was young. In truth, neither he nor his godfather could have felt much embarrassment, for they barely knew one another. 'We never had a special relationship,' said Christopher. 'He may have been standing round my cot but I can only recall seeing him twice in my life. He had been away playing cricket and then working in the City, just as I have been away from London and have only twice been able to see Paul Downton's daughter, my god-daughter.'

Not surprisingly, Christopher's appointment received enormous publicity. He was greeted with goodwill, a degree of optimism and, on account of his name, rather more publicity than would have been the norm. The enormity of his task was overlooked, even if the remedy for England's ills was as

171

*Godfather and England captain. The task ahead for May and Christopher is an onerous one. (*The Times *Photo Library)*

172

desperate as their circumstances. For Christopher had played in only a handful of Tests, and with minimal success. May's comments had fuelled the press even further: he was looking to the future and was billing Christopher's appointment as a new beginning. The series against West Indies was, after all, as good as lost. His hope was that Christopher would do well enough, without necessarily beating West Indies in the remaining two Tests, to captain England in the final Test of the summer against Sri Lanka and then lead them on the tour that winter to India. On his way to see May before the appointment, Christopher had telephoned his father: 'I'm going to see an old friend of yours,' he said.

It was a tonic for Colin, who again had not been well, but his pleasure was tempered with concern over the timing of the appointment. The protective father in him felt that, ideally, Christopher should not have been made captain until England played Sri Lanka. Instead, he was blooded against the strongest team in the world with little apparent chance of succeeding. The doubts that were raised over the selection of Christopher, be they by players or the media, had less to do with his captaincy – his supposedly weak Kent side was now 37 points clear of the pack – than his worth as batsman and bowler, and a suspicion in some quarters that he was chosen because of who he was and not what he was. For Christopher, such criticism was hackneyed, only the difference now was that it was not merely confined to Kent. What once might have been a topic for the *Kent Messenger* was an issue for the *Observer*. Would Christopher, it asked, have been made captain if his name had been John Smith or Simon Hinks (the Kent batsman)? Carol, Christopher's sister, found that at parties she attended there was discussion within earshot of Christopher Cowdrey the cricketer, not Christopher Cowdrey her brother. 'Before the Test people were saying he would be found out. Some only wanted to talk to me because I was a Cowdrey and I knew I had to be careful about what I said.' When she had heard of Christopher's appointment, she unashamedly burst into tears.

There was but a week between the announcement and the start of the fourth Test, which was to be at Headingley. For Christopher, it was pell-mell. The telephone rang constantly. When he put his answer phone on, it became near jammed with messages. The tabloid press focused on his blonde Swedish girlfriend, Christel Holst-Sande, who had moved into his Canterbury home. They had met in a pub the previous year on the same day that Christopher had made a guest appearance with David Gower, in the West End in 'Run for your Wife'. Although Christel's career had encompassed various activities (including a period as a classical singer), she was tagged a 'financial consultant', not least because she was already planning Christopher's benefit, due the following year. She knew little of cricket, but concentrated his mind by talking to him as if she were Peter May. Christel went with him to the cramped ground at Guildford, where Kent were playing Surrey prior to the Test, but there she was unable to be supportive. Players, wives, girlfriends, press and assorted hangers-on shared the same balcony, which did little for Christopher's peace of mind, let alone Christel's. Reporters conferred about Christopher in the row of seats behind her; photographers almost followed her into the lavatory. That same week, more photographers clambered into the kitchen of Penny's cottage in Limpsfield Chart; it stands, appropriately enough, in Grub Street. Christopher, meanwhile, was out without scoring in his last innings before the Test.

Stewart was on the ground during the match, yet, to Christopher's surprise, did not seek him out. For cricketing advice Christopher turned, at long last, to his father, having come to the opinion that no-one else knew as much about cricket or could impart their knowledge better. Colin had never subjected Christopher to his views if they were not sought, but once telephoned, he had many conversations with him in the days before the Test. Their relationship, while still not a close one, was based on mutual respect for each other as cricketers. Colin's name and achievements, initially conspicuous by their absence from *The Cricketers' Who's Who*, had long been installed by Christopher in the section marked 'family links with cricket' under Christopher's name.

Colin and Christopher were the second father and son pairing to lead England, the first having been F.T. and F.G. Mann. They had each won a series against South Africa, an achievement the Cowdreys would not be able to match against West Indies, even if Christopher won both the Tests for which he had been appointed. Indeed, there was little that was propitious. England had last used three captains in a series in 1966 – against West Indies. The series had been lost and the captaincy taken away from Colin. At Headingley that year he had had his car damaged after England had been beaten. When Christopher arrived in his car, on the eve of the Test, the gateman did not recognise him.

It did little for his confidence in preparation for the crucial team gathering later that day. As soon as the team meeting began, Graham Gooch stood up and told Christopher he was behind him. They were good friends. Of the England side that lost the third Test at Old Trafford, only Gooch, Gower – playing in his 100th Test – Lamb and Dilley remained. There was nothing distinctive about the selection to suggest that Christopher had had a particular influence. Athey, Pringle and Richards were recalled and Foster was fit again. In the two new caps, Curtis and Robin Smith, England had gone for players with a reputation for coping with fast bowling. Christopher's most awkward task thus far had been to tell Downton, an old friend, that he had been omitted. There was no spinner included, Emburey having been discarded; indeed, only three specialist bowlers played. If it was not exactly hoped that Christopher would provide the ballast, he was, as he had been in India, crucial to the balance of the side.

Neither Colin nor Penny could face watching their son: intrinsically they were too concerned for him. Penny had found it taxing enough to watch Colin in his pomp. Christel travelled to Leeds only to discover that the zoom lenses were to be trained on her as much as on Christopher. Carol and Jeremy, who dispelled his nerves by constantly checking the weather forecast, stayed with the family of Carol's husband of two years, Alastair Keith, a surveyor; they lived, conveniently, in Leeds.

The forecasts that Jeremy heard were, in fact, mixed. Rain fell on the Wednesday, the eve of the Test, and hard enough to flood the bowlers' run-ups. Play began 50 minutes late and was interrupted while problems over a drainage system were resolved. West Indies had won the toss, put England in and in due course were again in the ascendancy: England 80 for four. There followed perhaps the one period in the course of the summer when West Indies were, if not quite grovelling, down-trodden. Allan Lamb and Robin Smith, showing that he was a player for the future, put on 103 for the fifth wicket. It was a stand ended prematurely when Lamb hobbled off having pulled a calf muscle. England's innings never recovered. Smith and Christopher were out at the same score, Christopher lasting twelve balls without scoring before he was leg before to Malcolm Marshall. From 183 for four, England were all out for 201, Lamb not returning to bat. They were handicapped further when Dilley went off with a leg strain after eight overs, yet kept West Indies' total within reasonable proportions. At the close on the second day West Indies were 45 runs behind with five wickets intact and Christopher was up to joking with Marshall about his dismissal in the sponsors' tent. He appeared to be relaxed, swopping light-hearted banter and appreciating a joke Marshall played on Lamb, who appeared on crutches and, upon biting on a fake walnut, extracted only a condom. Later that evening Christopher dined with Tim Wright, who was without a car: Christopher thought nothing about collecting his girlfriend from the station.

On the Saturday, only 23 overs were possible, West Indies taking a lead of 37 for the loss of three more wickets. They were, at that stage, only marginal favourites to win a match in which they had to bat last on a pitch that was helping the seamers. Yet that lead was extended to 74 on the fourth morning and, in the context of a low-scoring match, it was a lot. England could muster only 138 in their second innings, no-one but Gooch, who made 50, contributing a score of note. Christopher's second innings lasted 36 balls and five runs before Walsh bowled him with a straight ball which he might have kept out had he played forward. West Indies won by ten wickets a match which would not have lasted three days had the drainage system worked properly and had it not rained.

It was a chastening experience for Christopher, which would have been only partially mitigated had the match been played at, say, Lord's or the Oval. He had looked uncomfortable throughout, as if in a daunting crucible. His England had lost, and yet that was almost to be expected. What was more disconcerting was his own form. His father thought he looked vulnerable technically; his bowling, and he had only 5.3 overs, was scathingly criticised on the air by Fred Trueman. He had re-discovered, too, the difference between County and Test cricket. 'The two games are so very far apart,' he said. 'I think I always knew that but one Test against this West Indies side strengthened my convictions. The championship is great fun to play and great fun to watch. The ball is flying about everywhere on sporty pitches, something is happening all the time and batsmen eventually decide they must chance their arm to survive. But from this system you have to find a team to play a much harsher form of cricket, on generally good pitches and against high-class fast bowling. It is a real dilemma.' He was to return to this theme when he posed the question, 'Should we spoil the fun?' in an article for *The Cricketer*. He rejoined Kent, who had benefited as much as any county from the poor pitches around the country, for the one championship match he would be able to participate in before the fifth Test at the Oval. It was Canterbury week, Kent's own festival. There was an England captain to celebrate, surely, in addition to an imminent championship pennant. But it all went horribly wrong.

Kent were beaten – thrashed – by Somerset, who won by an innings. Steve Waugh, then little known, scored a century of precocious brilliance. Only Graham, with a half-century, made a decent score for Kent. In their first innings Christopher had been hit on a foot by Adrian Jones, the Somerset fast bowler, and it was bruised sufficiently for him to have to bat at number eleven the following day. That was a Tuesday, two days before the fifth Test would start. That evening Stewart telephoned him and tried to make him pull out then and there.

The next day, the eve of the Test, the swelling had not gone down. Christopher withdrew and was replaced by Gooch, the only man to play in every Test that summer. Christopher was not, he thought, wanted at the Oval, even as a spectator – although nominally still England captain, Stewart's suggestion that he might appear during the match was, he felt, only half-hearted. Lamb, who was likewise injured, went to the ground, but then his place in the side was secure; had Christopher gone, it might have been interpreted that he was trying to cling on to his job. That was his dilemma: so he stayed at Canterbury and watched Kent's next match instead.

The long walk back. Christopher, lbw to Marshall for 0, is succeeded at the wicket by Jack Richards. (The Times *Photo Library)*

Gooch, as England's fourth captain of the summer, fared competently, even though another Test match was lost. His doggedly resolute second innings of 84, scored while wickets fell about him, emphasised that he was a captain who was worth his place in the side. He was duly appointed captain for the Test against Sri Lanka, even though Christopher was by now fit again, and subsequently for the tour to India.

On the day that Gooch was given the captaincy against Sri Lanka, Christopher was scoring a century against Derbyshire at Chesterfield at a run a ball. There was a difference of opinion as to his fitness: he claimed he was up to playing in a five-day Test, Stewart claimed he was not. 'He telephoned me to ask how I was and our views differed,' said Christopher. 'I could not believe people were saying that I wasn't fit. They should have been big enough to communicate, and I was not the first England captain during the summer to feel that way. One moment I was England captain and the next I had disappeared.'

Kent's match with Derbyshire was drawn but a victory over Hampshire the same week put them back at the top of the championship table. In a low-scoring affair on a pitch which helped the seam bowlers throughout, they achieved this in part through a fourth-wicket stand of 72 between Christopher and Tavaré that set up a declaration on the final day. Graham was now finding the form that had eluded him since early in the season, scoring half-centuries against Gloucestershire and Sussex. Neither match, though, had been won, merely adding to Christopher's frustration, for Worcestershire, with Graeme Hick rampant, were now clear challengers. Gloucestershire had three wickets in hand and were short of their target when bad light ended play four overs early. The final blow to Kent's title hopes, though, was their defeat in the four-day match against Sussex at Maidstone. Having put Sussex in and bowled them out for 184, Kent collapsed after a sound start and gained a first innings lead of only 49. They were eventually left needing 311 to win and, despite a partnership of 96 between Tavaré and Graham, unaccountably collapsed.

Stewart had maintained to Christopher that he would stay in contact, yet they had not spoken again. Christopher's agitation was in keeping with his character: if he is not given an immediate response, he will think he is not being given one at all. He was starting to say in public what he had been thinking in private. He had already made his views known to a group of journalists during Kent's match with Hampshire at Bournemouth – they did not report them since they were drinking with him at a bar at the time – when he was approached by Ian Todd, a journalist on *The Sun*, during a benefit game at the H.A.C ground in London at the end of August. Todd had come ostensibly to see him to talk about Kent and their hopes of winning the championship, and soon found, after lobbing in one or two questions about England, that he had a story. Christopher, for his part, was wise enough in the ways of the tabloid press to know that anything he said would be on the back page the next morning. What he told Todd had been welling up: here was a platform to get it off his chest. He even had an unavowed liking for *The Sun*.

He told Todd that he had written to May, telling him he was not available to go to India. 'England can stick tour job' was the headline (which he thought was mis-leading: it looked as if he had said that, and it upset May and Stewart). 'After the shabby way the selectors have treated me, I'd rather forget about the tour and concentrate on leading Kent to the championship. Then I just want to take a complete break from cricket,' he said.

'After the big build-up I got when they appointed me, I'm still waiting to be told where I went wrong or why I wasn't good enough after just one match at Headingley. A call would be appreciated, even now. But it's too late to change the way I feel. I was built up by the chairman of selectors as a captain whose enthusiasm and bubble would rub off on the rest of the team and perhaps give us a new fighting spirit. What they wanted to see was a different attitude, a new fighting spirit as I settled into the job. Then, if things went well against Sri Lanka, we would have something to build on for the Indian tour this winter.

'I don't believe I was such a failure at Headingley, though that's something I have to accept if that's what the selectors believe. I may not like to be told I'm not a good enough player at Test level or that I haven't, after all, got the leadership qualities the selectors are looking for. But I deserve, and I expect, an explanation about where I went wrong. It has all been a terrible let-down and I now feel I am struggling to maintain that enthusiasm and bubble.'

The quotes were dramatised in *Sun* style, but they were accurate. Christopher had nothing further to add when other newspapers attempted to follow up the story, which was as well since the T.C.C.B. fined him £500 at a subsequent disciplinary hearing (*The Sun*, which had not paid him for the interview, paid the fine). Christopher accepted he had contravened regulations about making statements without official consent and apologised.

Nonetheless, there was widespread sympathy for him, not least from his family – 'I saw one hell of a broken man,' said Carol – and the Kent chairman, Peter Edgley, who commended him for his honesty. Christopher, Woodhouse and a solicitor discussed the T.C.C.B.'s fine. 'Had it been any bigger and I had had to pay, we'd have dug the whole business up,' said Christopher a year later. 'My grouse was that I had not been talked to as an ordinary human being – and I still haven't.' In *The Cricketer*, Woodcock wrote that the selectors had treated Christopher 'like a dog'. Martin Johnson, *The Independent*'s cricket correspondent, saw the funny side: 'Christopher's present from the godfather turned out to be a burst from that branch of the family specialising in black homburgs and violin cases.' Colin, needless to say, was distressed at the publicity. May, after all, was one of his closest cricketing friends.

May was to retire from the chairmanship of the selectors just three months later. His friendship with Colin remained intact: they still met at functions and in committee. As sensitive to press criticism as Colin, May was inevitably hurt by his godson's comments, although he said he had not read them. A year later he thought the outburst had been made not by Christopher but by Christel. May was not fond of the media, be it as captain or chairman of selectors: in 1988 he took the *Daily Telegraph* as much for the crossword as for the cricket coverage. He was bemused by the modern trend of the captain giving interviews in the dressing-room. He felt that 'there was a greater loyalty to the system or the club in the past'. And he especially disliked the use of quotes. 'In my day the media commented on the cricket,' he said.

'I can't imagine myself coming out with the kind of remarks Christopher was alleged to have made. We gave him a chance and he didn't take it either as captain or with his performance. It doesn't help if I tell too many half-truths but the whole thing was too much for him, as we noticed off the field. It is never easy playing West Indies and he put his head underground. Mickey [Stewart] made it quite clear to him what our thinking was.'

It would not have been in Colin's nature to speak out in the manner Christopher had done: his public utterances, for one who has held positions of responsibility in the game for three decades, have been remarkably few. Once, Stuart Chiesman, annoyed by Colin's refusal to give a comment in his capacity as England captain, provided the press with one on his behalf. Les Ames could not recall him, throughout their long association, giving vent to his feelings. Even when he was passed over for the England captaincy in favour of Illingworth, he retreated into himself, his form and his peace of mind shattered. Colin had wider ambitions within the game. Christopher, by expressing his feelings verbally, would not have helped his prospects of furthering his career in the way his father has done. Not that that was uppermost in his ambitions, anyway. What was, was winning the championship.

Colin wrote in *M.C.C.* that 'Cricket was a mistress never to be taken for granted, she gave me her richest prizes and her cruellest lessons.' So it was now for Christopher. His injury could so easily have been a blessing – he would have avoided being blamed for a second defeat by West Indies and would have then returned as captain to defeat Sri Lanka. Then the captaincy for India would have been his. The capricious selectors saw it differently. They had proclaimed that England had required a leader of Christopher's calibre, yet, very soon, were behaving as if nothing of the sort had been said. Stewart, as he showed before and afterwards, was happiest working with a captain of like attitude and background to himself: a believer in meritocracy, he was clearly more attuned to Gooch and Gatting than to Gower and Cowdrey.

Shorn of the England captaincy, Christopher would have felt that winning the championship would be more than mere consolation. Above all else, he had wanted to captain Kent.

Now, there was another issue rankling with him, and with his county. When, in mid-summer, Kent beat Warwickshire at Edgbaston, they gained only three bonus bowling points instead of the maximum of four since they could take only eight first-innings wickets. Warwickshire had two batsmen injured. The T.C.C.B. said that the fourth point could be gained only when the ninth wicket fell. It aggravated Kent at the time, but it became only truly significant at the end of the season. They failed to beat Middlesex at Lord's (Graham scored 86) and were unable to gain a fourth batting bonus point as a result of a slow start. They obtained maximum points in their last match, against Surrey, and promptly opened the champagne. For a few hours, they were champions. Later that day news reached them that Worcestershire, by beating Glamorgan, had leap-frogged over them and won the championship – by a single point. That missing point from the match at Edgbaston now took on considerable significance; but the ruling stood. 'Oh, well, we'll make something of it,' Christopher joked to Mark Nicholas, looking ahead to his year as Kent's beneficiary. 'The pointless benefit dinner, perhaps!'

Christopher maintained that Kent's success in finishing runners-up was, considering the relative paucity of talent, 'the greatest achievement in this club's history'. His own batting had been indifferent. His bowling, which brought him 39 wickets, and Graham's batting, although he had still to reach 1,000 runs in a season, had been components in Kent's success. Graham played in eighteen championship matches, scoring 790 runs and averaging 31. Kent were pipped by what, on paper as in reality, was a stronger side, and yet in all but the experimental four-day matches they had played compelling cricket. Christopher's captaincy had been the keystone to their success.

Having ruled himself out of the tour to India – which ultimately did not take place – Christopher was able to devote himself to preparing for his benefit, granted ten years after he had won his county cap. His father spurned a benefit; when he started in the game, only a professional cricketer took one. Carol, for one, felt that Graham would also shy away from it through embarrassment when his turn came. Jeremy thought differently. Christopher, for all his extroversion, found it hard

Christopher and Christel, after their marriage at the Swedish church in Marylebone on New Year's Day. Gower was best man. (The Press Association)

to ask his friends for contributions, even in the form of tickets for dinners or dances.

Carol and Jeremy gave Christopher substantial help with the preparation; and so, of course, did Christel. A year younger than Christopher, she managed his life energetically, and turned into a home a house that had seemed to exist to provide digs for various Kent players. Bright and well-read, able to speak six languages and altogether proud of her Swedish heritage, she was highly ambitious for Christopher. She did not, though, regard herself as 'part of the Cowdrey dynasty', as she was introduced once in a speech by Graham Johnson. She was not amused. She knew that, with any realistic hopes of Christopher's playing again for England scattered by the selectors and his comments to *The Sun*, it would be possible for him just to drift through the remaining years of his career. Christel was intent on harnessing his energies so that this would not happen – and that he would in due course develop a life beyond cricket.

They were engaged that October, on Christopher's 31st birthday, and married on New Year's Day 1989 at the Swedish church in Marylebone, London. David Gower was best man and suggested to Graham that he take a bat to the reception to joke to the Swedish contingent that it was Christopher's first benefit function. All Christopher's family attended what was a small wedding of 100 guests. These did not include Peter May. He had not been invited.

The *Daily Telegraph* carried on their front page the next morning a photograph of Christopher and Gower flanking Christel, who wore a small gold crown, as is traditional at Swedish weddings. For their honeymoon, by necessity a short one since a benefit year is all-embracing, they went to Vienna, and to opera and ballet. 'I loved it,' said Christopher. 'I should never have considered doing those things ten years ago. Sport used to come above all else for me, but that's changing as I get older. I'd far rather have gone to a football match in the past.

'I felt the need to settle down and was lucky to meet the right person. If I'd married the girls I liked in my early 'twenties I'd have taken a chance. It would have gone wrong because I've matured and changed.'

Chapter Eleven

The Lure of the Rand

L ONG BEFORE CHRISTOPHER took his 1989 benefit, cricketers had come to realise that such a form of remuneration,
however outmoded, could be substantially commercialised.
Once upon a time the professional cricketer's team of helpers
ambled their way around County grounds with limited ambitions: the collecting buckets were filled and the beneficiary
was designated a match and its takings at the gate. Fund-raising
functions would be confined to within the county.

Christopher's benefit would clearly be rather different. He
had not just a chairman of his benefit committee (Derek
Ufton) but an executive chairman (Paul Box-Grainger). The
foreword to a glossy brochure packed with local and national
advertising was written by Denis Thatcher on Downing Street
notepaper. A Kent sportsman himself, he wrote that 'to follow
so outstanding a cricket father as Colin Cowdrey calls for
character, courage and enthusiasm, and Chris has displayed
all these qualities in his career'. Colin contributed the longest
article, recalling a conversation two young Kent members had
had about the Cowdreys when, unknowingly, they were seated
at the same table as him in the new stand at Canterbury (likely,
ultimately, to be named the Cowdrey stand). The conversation
was fairly complimentary. There were family photographs
provided by Carol. All that went askew in the brochure,
printed by Box-Grainger's firm, was a caption which depicted
the dog as Carol. As to the functions, there were numerous
events in Kent and the West End. There was a £55 a head ball
at the Mayfair Hotel and two trips on the Orient Express.

The benefit year began in January, and not on the ideal
footing. Having been fined by the T.C.C.B. only the previous
month, Christopher was intent on maintaining a low profile.
He abandoned the idea of writing a review of the 1988 season
in *The Times*, which would have appeared at Christmas. He
would have to make a number of speeches in the year ahead

Graham, Colin, Christopher and Jeremy at Tunbridge Wells for Kent v Old Kent in 1988. (The Times Photo Library)

and keep a balance between opinion and discretion: it was important to him that any strictures on English cricket should not be reported.

The launch took the form of a lunch at the Great Danes Hotel near Maidstone that went on until early evening. Christopher had given a ticket to the Kent chairman, Peter Edgley, who was also joint managing director of the *Kent Messenger*, the leading newspaper in the county. Edgley sent instead a reporter who, unbeknown to Christopher, was planning to write it up. In the following week's edition some comments repeating what he had said in *The Sun* were splashed across the back page. This was the start of a series of difficulties Christopher had with the *Kent Messenger*, which, Edgley's position notwithstanding, was quite prepared to be critical of him and, especially, Jim Woodhouse, who was now Kent's chief executive.

So Christopher, complete with signet ring when he reported back for pre-season training, would not be drawn at their press day on anything other than Kent's prospects for the forthcoming season. Tavaré having departed after his own benefit, his pride still wounded, Christopher was the oldest person on the staff. Optimistically, he felt that Kent had not yet realised their full potential. He knew, though, that it was important to find a person of the stature and knowledge of John Inverarity to impart specialist coaching. Inverarity, having taken up a headmastership in Australia, was unavailable; hence Christopher turned to his father.

Colin had not then been appointed for a second term at I.C.C. and was involved in only a part-time capacity at Barclays. He had also shed two stone; Christopher and Graham followed the same diet. He assisted with pre-season coaching in the nets at Canterbury and in particular helped Mark Benson immeasurably, impressing upon him the need to stay in line against fast bowling. As a result, this aspect of Benson's game was much improved: he averaged over 50 and came close to regaining an England place that had been his for just one Test. Colin did continue to do some coaching but not on a regular basis. For one thing, he lived too far from Canterbury; for another, he was too involved in cricket at Arundel. But he retained his place on the committee and his influence within the club.

He was soon immersed in wider aspects of the game. In mid-July 1989 he was appointed chairman of I.C.C., his aims much as they were when he chaired their annual meeting as President of M.C.C. Now, though, he had a term of four years in which to curb bouncers, restore the art of spin bowling and make progress towards an international panel of umpires. The T.C.C.B.'s attempts to reduce the permissible number of bouncers to one per over were not looked upon favourably at the I.C.C. meeting during the summer. 'Of all the challenges Cowdrey has faced, his assignment at I.C.C. will be as tough as any,' wrote Christopher Martin-Jenkins in an editorial for *The Cricketer.* His friendship with Clyde Walcott, newly elected President of West Indies Cricket Board, was likely to be put to the test. West Indies were in a minority in wishing to have no limit to the number of bouncers bowled other than when they amounted to intimidation. For, of course, they had too many exceptionally fast bowlers to want to tinker with the laws. Colin's task, as he set out to converse with cricketing bodies all around the world – he aimed to visit every country where there was a Test match played in 1990 – was to encourage them to experiment.

When Colin took office in October 1989, he had an unappealing task to carry out. On 1 August, the final day of the fourth Test, it was disclosed that sixteen cricketers under the leadership of Mike Gatting would tour South Africa that winter and the following year. Among those names which Colin listed as ineligible for Test cricket for those two years, and then for a further five, was that of Christopher. At the age of 31 his Test career was now certainly over, if it had not been already.

Christopher was playing for Kent against Worcestershire when the news broke. A year before, the two counties had been vying with each other for leadership of the championship; now, with Worcestershire top, Kent were losing this match and were to start Canterbury week at the bottom of the table. Christopher's own form had been patchy; the demands of the benefit and, perhaps, the clandestine way in which the tour had been set up, told on his form. It was to improve dramatically thereafter, even though he and Richard Ellison had to contend with anti-apartheid placards upon arrival at the St. Lawrence ground, Canterbury, for the remainder of the season.

189

Back at the crease . . . Colin, recovered from his operation, prepares to take guard for Old Kent in his 57th year. (The Times Photo Library)

The uniform press statement handed to the media at Worcester that morning was written in Christopher's hand on behalf of himself, Ellison and Graham Dilley. It was to the effect that they were going to South Africa as professional sportsmen and were not condoning the regime there. There had been a report earlier in the summer, which Christopher had denied, that he would be captaining an unofficial England tour. This was before Gatting joined, and such a choice would have made sense: quite apart from his flair for public relations, Christopher's surname alone was a sure-fire attraction to South Africans, who in isolation inevitably live out the past. That he was also the son of the incoming chairman of I.C.C. would have made his appointment as captain of the 'rebels' a major coup for Ali Bacher.

Christopher consulted friends as to whether he should go to South Africa. He also considered the moral implications. He had to weigh up that and how it might affect his benefit, with the huge financial rewards. He did not discuss it with his father. 'But it will not cause any problems,' he said. 'I hope it will not create any difficulties with Kent, either, since I have every intention of continuing to play County cricket.' He had met Bacher in April in London and was told of the coaching programme the South African Cricket Union was undertaking in the townships. 'We did not discuss money at all. He wanted to try to find out who would go, collected the names of various individuals and went back to see sponsors in South Africa. I had already made up my mind that I was keen to join.'

It was in the knowledge that he was highly unlikely to play for England again, and that he would receive £83,000 tax free (the tax was to be paid by S.A.C.U.) that he signed what was intended to be a watertight contract for two tours. No player was supposed to talk to the press until twelve months after the second tour. If that was untenable, the identities of the players in the party being assembled were more or less successfully withheld until the news was officially released.

Christopher had no immediate plans for retirement, but he was aware he had reached the last leg of his career as a sportsman. He was finding it harder to keep fit and felt that he would be unable to continue until he was 40. 'It used to be possible to carry on, but nowadays, with so much playing

191

and travelling, people burn themselves out more quickly.' His friends were aware that he was looking to the future and that he no longer placed sport above everything else. He was endeavouring to see more of his family than he had in the past and was talking, loosely, of owning a company with sporting connections after retiring from cricket.

The Kent committee's reaction to his going to South Africa was not exactly positive. The captaincy was reviewed annually and there was some debate as to whether Christopher, now effectively an overseas player, should continue. It was not long, either, since the committee had been displeased by his comments in *The Sun*. Colin, while not embarrassed by Christopher's going to South Africa and naturally wanting the best for him as his son, felt in his capacity as chairman of I.C.C. that as Christopher was now ineligible for England, for him to continue as the Kent captain would not be for the good of English cricket. But there was no other apparent leader on Kent's staff (with the exception of Graham); and Christopher was duly appointed captain for 1990, a decision which contrasted sharply with the committee's dismissal of Asif Iqbal for joining World Series Cricket in 1977 – as Asif, who likes Christopher, pointed out. (In 1977 Asif was upset since Colin, he felt, had been party to his dismissal after seemingly accepting his reasons for joining WSC.) In addition, Asif said, South Africa was a moral issue.

The committee's other concern, unsurprisingly, was Kent's poor season. Both matches in Canterbury week were lost to weak opponents and Kent finished just ten points above the bottom-placed county, Glamorgan. This in spite of five batsmen finishing the season with more than 1,000 runs, Christopher included. His form had picked up from the moment his winter plans were revealed: in the last six and a half weeks of the season he scored 56 against Worcestershire; 56 against Warwickshire; 57 and 53 off Glamorgan; an unbeaten 146 from 152 balls off Surrey, his highest score of the season; 69 against Middlesex. His championship average, 37, was his highest since 1983.

It was the bowling which let Kent down. Christopher himself took only twelve championship wickets. The leading wicket taker, Alan Igglesden, had just 53. In the Sunday

League Kent slipped from seventh to twelfth place. Only in the Benson and Hedges Cup did they excel, losing to Nottinghamshire in the semi-finals after an exciting victory over Northamptonshire in their quarter-final. Through it all Christopher continued to transmit the impression that cricket was fun. Yet as with every county that experiences a lean season, there were some malcontents. Some of the players, it seemed, were irked by the publicity which continued to engulf the Cowdreys.

For Graham, it had been an unexceptional season. Christopher had felt that, with the spur of being awarded his county cap and having had a break from the game in the winter of 1988–89, he was on the verge of consistent form. Yet he played in just eight championship matches, scoring 153 runs, of which 108 came in one innings against Leicestershire. It was a determined and courageous century, since he was palpably out of form and the ball was not coming on to the bat. As before, he was seen at his best in the one-day game. At Folkestone, a week after the *Mail on Sunday* had run a story stating that he would be sacked at the end of the season, he made an unbeaten 102 off 76 balls against a useful Leicestershire attack in a Sunday match. It was a savage innings, full of big hitting.

The *Mail on Sunday* report was inaccurate and, besides, a curt notice of dismissal would not be the method by which Kent would rid themselves of a Cowdrey. Colin wrote in *M.C.C.* that he shrank from the possibility towards the end of his career that he might be taken on to a golf course and given a gentle hint that it might be time to finish. There was a grain of truth in the *Mail on Sunday*'s report, for there was some concern, notably among the coaching staff, as to Graham's commitment to the game. Nevertheless, the committee maintained the belief that Graham, now 25, possessed sufficient talent: it was a question of whether he could express it. He himself felt he had not had a decent run in the team; he had, too, been injured for five weeks of the season.

'If he can stay in for fifteen overs he has as much ability as anyone in the Kent side,' said Bill Sale, a committee member and his former headmaster. 'He is desperate to succeed and if he doesn't he is furious with no-one but himself.' The club would not, though, stand in his way if he wanted to leave

A trinity of former England captains . . . and rebels. Emburey, Gatting and Christopher, South Africa-bound, opposed in a one-day match at Lord's. (The Times *Photo Library*)

and, indeed, his name was linked with Middlesex during the autumn. It was nothing new, in one sense, since there had been suggestions, rumours and counter-rumours that he might move to another county since he was seventeen. Ever since, hypothetical arguments had gone on as to whether he would have benefited from playing at a different county under a tough captain who adhered to rigorous practice; but then much the same had been said about Christopher. 'How do you make the break without letting down others?' said Joffy Sale, Bill's son and a friend from prep and public school. 'There is pressure on him from people within the county, from those who taught him at Tonbridge. They expect a lot.'

194

Graham knew that it would be less difficult to make the break from his brother. Neither he nor Christopher had found their relationship during the summer months an easy one. 'It is far harder to play for a brother as captain than to captain a brother,' said Christopher. In 1989 he deferred to Woodhouse over selection of Graham, who wrote in Christopher's benefit brochure: 'We have formed a fairly set routine. In the summer we have a fairly tight formal relationship although obviously Chris remains a brother and a great friend; but he's also my boss so there has to be some distance left between us. In the winter when the pressure is off, it is a lot easier to have a normal brother to brother relationship. I have no real personal ambitions in cricket but I would like to think I could leave the game with as many friends and supporters as Chris has made during his career.'

That autumn, Graham was not the only individual within Kent C.C.C. having to consider where his future lay. To the chagrin of Christopher and, especially, of Colin, the committee decided not to renew Woodhouse's contract as chief executive, a post he was combining with chairing the cricket committee. In the round he lacked tact, which upset others on the 27-man committee, the chairman included. Yet Christopher and the Kent players liked and respected him. He was an effective buffer between them and the committee.

Colin was wearisome at the committee meeting in question that October evening. He had taken over at I.C.C. and retained his roles on other committees, notably with sub-committees of the Skinners company. He was a governor of Tonbridge School which the Skinners, a City guild, had set up. He had become accustomed to employing a driver to ferry him to and from his various meetings so that he could take a nap beforehand or afterwards, hence perpetuating the nickname 'Kipper' which had been bestowed upon him in his playing days. Whether or not he had slept on the way to Canterbury, Colin was disconcerted that his support for Woodhouse was not shared by a majority of the Kent committee. Colin had initially been behind his appointment as chairman of the cricket committee; he saw him as someone who might re-structure the club and, perhaps, protect Christopher's back. Colin made the point that there was nothing like the same criticism of Kent when he began under David Clark though Clark's side had been no more successful. But it was to no avail. Sensing that Woodhouse was not wanted, Colin gathered his papers and, to the astonishment of the remainder of the committee, walked out in a huff.

There were aspersions, too, that the votes of Woodhouse and Christopher were not cast, hence affecting the outcome – which was that Woodhouse resigned before completing his first year as chief executive. Neither he nor Christopher had been at the meeting. The structure of administration was complicated further when later Woodhouse was re-elected chairman of the cricket committee while Kent contemplated seeking a new chief executive.

After Woodhouse's contract was not renewed, James Capel decided not to continue with their sponsorship of Kent, which was worth £25,000 a year. In addition they contributed a further £5,000 per annum for equipment and offered the county £5,000 for each trophy they won. So the whole package could have brought Kent £50,000 a year. In reality it did not exceed £30,000 since Kent did not win any of the four competitions during the four years of sponsorship. James Capel took the view that it was time for a change, but added significantly that they were surprised Kent had parted with Woodhouse. Jeremy was still at the firm: he had become a senior executive and in May had married Pippa Telford, a City fund manager. Graham, on a rare day free from cricket, was best man, and made an acclaimed speech.

In the autumn of 1989 Graham undertook a tour of Barbados with a side run by Fred Rumsey, the England bowler turned travel agent. In the winter he flew to Perth, to be coached by Inverarity, his guru, and to help run the cricket at his school. 'You are a superb hitter of the ball,' Inverarity would impress upon Graham. 'Go out there and hit it.' There were times when he did. Christopher welcomed his decision to have a refresher. 'It could be the turning point for Graham,' he said.

Before leaving for South Africa (he hardly played on the ill-fated tour), Christopher himself was on the move – to a new home at Chartham, close to Canterbury. He and Christel had both been keen to leave Wincheap, which was not the most attractive area of Canterbury. They celebrated their first wedding anniversary in the coach house they had bought, which was set in the grounds of a larger house. Christopher's benefit was now over; the coffers were filling; with that and his South African plunder, he would be some £200,000 better off. (Those who would spend it for him, certain Old Tonbridgians, he kept at arm's length.) There were in 1989 Kent players who felt he should not have accepted a benefit: was he not a Cowdrey, does he not belong to the Mark McCormack organisation (if only in a minor way), was not his grandfather Stuart Chiesman? Yet the Cowdreys are not hoarders. Chiesman was a generous man who both made and spent his money, and the Cowdreys have followed suit. Penny and Ann were left comfortably off and trust funds were set up for the four children with capital accrued from the sale of the seven Chiesman stores, ultimately to House of Fraser. The joint proprietor's immediate legacy, a property in Sandwich, enabled them to buy homes of their own, albeit not in the most desirable parts of London.

History, it would seem, will judge the Cowdreys in much the same light as contemporaries view them now. Leaf through virtually any book written by a cricketer who played with or against Colin and the verdict is much the same. 'If only he had believed in himself . . . .' 'If he had had Peter May's determination . . . .' and so on. Ultimately such comments, however interesting they may be to read, are self-defeating. With Christopher, 'It was always unlikely that he would be as good as Colin Cowdrey, who possessed a gift for games that bordered on genius . . . .' 'If anything keeps him in the Test side it will be his spirit . . . .' In 100 years' time all the Cowdreys will be subject to a harsher scrutiny of facts and figures than they are today. There will still be clips of Colin's cover drive, Christopher's foxgrove hoick and Graham's short-arm pull, yet the statistics, as much as the contemporaneous writings, will be all important. Opinion is free; centuries, runs, catches, Test appearances are sacred.

Did Colin fulfil his potential? 'He made more of his gifts than most of us,' said John Woodcock. He was, though, lavishly endowed with them. *Wisden*, as ever, has to act as the ultimate arbitrator in assessing his place in the pantheon of batsmen. His Test average, 44.06, is that of a very good cricketer. Of his distinguished English contemporaries, Graveney matches it (44.38). May (46.77), Dexter (47.89) and Barrington (58.67) exceed it. Against Australia, the ultimate test before the West Indies became all-devouring, Colin averaged just 34.26; and of his four hundreds in ten series the highest was 113. Only one of these was made in a series in England. He was out between 100 and 115 more often than any other cricketer who scored a remotely comparable number of Test hundreds; that and his shortage of really big scores in County cricket can only be attributed to a lack of motivation once an initial challenge had been surmounted. For Kent and England, he was primarily a match-saving rather than a match-winning batsman. And the paradoxical nature of his batting is shown by sequences of low scores followed by a brilliant innings at a time when all semblance of form seemed to have deserted him.

As a captain, he himself says he should have clinched the succession in 1961, when May was injured and on the verge of retirement. Later, when Dexter stood for Parliament in 1964, Colin was the obvious person to succeed him. Yet the England selectors, chaired by Walter Robins, who had scant regard for his leadership, turned instead to Smith – who had not played for England during the summer of 1964. He had, though, taken M.C.C. to India in 1963 (when Colin was unable to lead them owing to injury). From then on, a combination of Colin's unassertive personality and ill-luck meant that the captaincy was rarely his for long. His sensitivity and cautious nature, accentuated by despondent circumstances when he assumed the captaincy of Kent and being regarded as England's perpetual deputy, did not suit him for the role. If he was a more decisive captain in the West Indies in 1967–68, his greatest tour, he was far less convincing in Pakistan the following winter. The injury which deprived Colin of the captaincy in 1969 was cruelly timed indeed. Yet had he established himself more firmly as England's captain earlier in the 1960s, it is likely that Illingworth, despite his success in 1970, would not have retained the captaincy for Australia in 1970–71. That tour was the final blow for Colin: Illingworth's achievements meant that never again would he be a contender for the captaincy of England.

The difficulties that Colin's sons would have in following him as first-class cricketers were encapsulated by one of several peculiarly insensitive remarks made to Christopher in the early years of his career. 'Why don't you hit the ball through the covers like your father?' 'If I could,' he said, 'I would.' Yet his surname, a hindrance to him then – and previously, at school – was a help to him later on. He knew that he would not be as good as his father; he hoped, by playing to his strengths, that he should be, in his own words, good enough. The comparisons dogged and affected him until he was an accomplished cricketer in his own right and both played for and captained England. Given that he had no exceptional talent, he has achieved about as much as he could have hoped to have done, however disappointing his tenure as England captain proved to be. As Kent's captain he has fulfilled his ambition; and whereas Colin led through his example with the bat, Christopher enthuses others through his ebullience and sheer love of cricket—and of life.

For Graham, the surname has been truly a mixed blessing. Cricket was not a calling. He possesses the ability and the determination to succeed while being still unconvinced as to whether cricket is really the career for him. His commitment is not absolute. He remains, even more than his father and brother, a private member of a very public family, one that was destined for renown from the moment when Ernest Cowdrey whimsically chose famous initials for his only son on an isolated tea plantation on the sub-continent.

Index